The

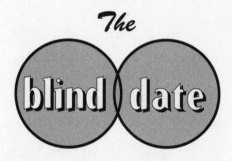
blind date

Guide to Dating

The

blind date

Guide to Dating

Frank Thompson

St. Martin's Griffin
New York

For Claire—
Every day with you is like
the best possible blind date.

www.stmartins.com

Book design by Jane Adele Regina

Library of Congress Cataloging-in-Publication Data

Thompson, Frank T.
    The Blind Date guide to dating / Frank Thompson.
       p. cm.
    ISBN 0-312-28660-0
    1. Blind dates. 2. Dating (Social customs). 3. Man-woman relationships. I. Blind Date (Television program). II. Title.

HQ801 .T475 2001
646.7'7–dc21   2001048235

First Edition: November 2001

10 9 8 7 6 5 4 3 2 1

Contents

Foreword

I remember it like it was yesterday. Back in 1999, I was having dinner with my friends John and Rebecca on a very cold and rainy night in Woodland Hills, California. I mentioned to them during sushi that I was in the running to host a new dating show and that the format was really different from anything else I had ever done before. They were very excited for me. So after dinner we headed back to my place to view a copy of the pilot episode the producers had given me. What happened next I will never forget. After watching for no more than thirty seconds, John got up and headed for the door.

"Where are you going?" I asked. "Don't you want to watch?"

"I don't have to," he replied. "This show is going to be a hit, and you'd be stupid not to host it."

And with that piece of advice, they were out the door.

I have to admit, I agreed with my friend. While previous dating shows were about winning the date or discussing a date that had already taken place, *Blind Date* wanted to shoot the actual date as it unfolded. Which of course meant that we would capture everything on videotape. How uncomfortable! How embarrassing! How entertaining!

Hosting *Blind Date* has been nothing but a constant adventure and an amazing exploration into human behavior. Just when I think I have seen it all, someone comes along and leaves me shaking my head in disbelief. I mean, who could ever forget Jeremy? This clown stripped down stark naked in a last-ditch effort to get his date's phone number. Trust me, guys, if your date wants to see you naked, she'll let you know. Or how about David? We all watched in horror as this Prince Charming decided to intention- ally pass gas during the cab ride home not once, but three times! Gee, I'm shocked he's single.

People ask me all the time which dates I like best. I have to ad- mit, my favorite dates are the ones that go well and the couple ac- tually takes the time to get to know one another. I guess it's the old-fashioned romantic in me, but when things go smoothly and our couples continue to date each other, it's kind of nice to know that we're responsible for that.

I have now watched and commented on over a thousand dates, and while I certainly don't claim to be a professional, I have learned a thing or two about the all-important first date and the dating dynamics between a man and a woman. I can't wait to share with you all that I have observed and learned in my upcom- ing book, which will be hitting bookstores very soon. In the mean- time, I hope you enjoy this book. It's a lot of fun!

It has been so exciting for me to be a small part of *Blind Date*'s success, and I would like to thank each and every one of you who tune in to our show. Thanks so much for making us America's #1 dating program. We are truly grateful.

God bless,
Roger Lodge
August 2001

Introduction

Almost everybody has been through it at least once. That long, tension-filled walk to the door; the thrill of anticipation—or the trickle of dread—that on the other side of that door will be your dream come true—or your worst nightmare. The second thoughts, the panicked urge to get out while the getting's good. Even as you ring the doorbell, a small, sane voice in the back of your mind is telling you to run away and don't look back.

But then the door opens and, for better or worse, your blind date is underway. And now all you can do is ride it out and hope you survive.

The blind date as a social convention goes all the way back to the days when dating first began gaining popularity—oh, let's say, 1761. Although other traditions from that era, like public whippings and witch burnings, have virtually died out in at least forty-eight of the United States, the cruel spectacle of the blind date lives on.

Traditionally, the blind date comes about when two singles are set up by well-meaning sadists, um, friends who either truly believe that they have found the perfect match for the pair, or are so miserable in their own relationships that they just want to make sure that the pain has been spread around as much as possible. Sometimes these so-called friends actually come along on the date, so that they can gloat and snicker and embarrass the blind daters later, and for the rest of their lives.

Today, through incredible advances in technology, singles can now set themselves up on their own blind dates through the e-mail, Internet chat rooms, personals columns, or random crank phone calls. These dates often work out marginally better than the other kind, simply because both daters have at least some idea of what the other is like, due to the huge lies they have told each other in e-mails and on the phone. The sad part is that, without the participants of the matchmakers, there is no one along for the ride to laugh at the pain and discomfort of the blind date couple when their date really starts to go south.

At least there wasn't until the hit television show *Blind Date* came along. Now, at long last, hopeful couples can not only go out on blind dates, but they can have their experiences interpreted by thought-bubble producers and enjoyed by millions of viewers around the U.S. and Canada. Now that's progress!

Blind Date was the brainchild of Jay Renfroe and David Garfinkle of Gold Coast Television and producer Thomas Klein. Klein recalls, "The idea really first came about over lunch one day when David and I started discussing the idea of creating a dating/relationship show that was actually based as much on comedy as it was on dating. We were fascinated with the idea of creating a 'next generation' dating show that took the dating concept out of the studio and really into the laps of the viewers."

Before *Blind Date*, nearly all television dating shows had been studio-based, where the daters simply talked about their experiences. Renfroe, Garfinkle, and Klein believed it would be much more fun to actually go along on the date as opposed to just hearing about it after the fact.

At the time, Gold Coast was producing a comedy show called *Fast Food Films.* This half-hour program took three low-budget films and made-for-TV movies, cut each one down to six minutes and, with added narration, graphics, and dubbed-in dialogue, turned it into something else—and something funnier. David Garfinkle believed that a similar process would be fun for a dating show. He recalls, "I thought it would be really cool if we took a whole date, edited it down to just a few minutes and made something really funny out of it—essentially turn the date into a fast food film."

They found a man and woman who were willing to be set up on a televised blind date and videotaped the entire event—which weighed in at around twelve hours. Renfroe was given the task of boiling all that footage down to a few entertaining minutes. But the date itself wasn't funny at all. He remembers, "It was so depressing, so painful to watch. I just sat in the edit room and thought, 'Why would anybody do this and why would anybody want to watch?' I went back to David and Tom and said, 'We'll never sell this. It's just too depressing to watch people on a blind date. We have to come up with something that makes it more entertaining or we're going to be responsible for a lot of people jumping off bridges and slitting their wrists after watching this thing.'"

But then inspiration struck, "I was watching the footage," Renfroe recalls, "and at one point I thought, 'Man, she is just so done with this guy and she's not saying it and he's not getting it! He is in complete denial of the real truth of the situation.'" Suddenly, he had an idea. "I said, 'We can do it all with graphics,'" Renfroe remembered. "I wanted to make the date look like a comic strip but keep the daters real and their story real. I said, 'We can create humorous thought bubbles that really communicate what they're thinking and we can use other graphics to help the audience understand the crucial moments in the date—why they're connecting or why this is a train wreck—and why am I having so much fun watching this couple crash and burn?' I put a couple of jokes over the most painful scenes and it worked. It was a perfect blend of reality and comedy."

Because of that blend, *Blind Date* was more than just another dating show. It was a subtextual viewing experience where the audience received layers of information about the two people on a date. "We thought there was so much unspoken that went on when two people were on a date," Klein says. "So we borrowed somewhat from the commercial world, which creates information on a multilayered level, by creating thought bubbles, and graphic icons to give the audience both insight and comedy about the two people. These story-telling devices really set *Blind Date* apart from what had been done on television up to that point."

In order to make sure that the show was insightful as well as funny, psychologist Michael Gold was brought on board to serve as "Therapist Joe." (By the way, Therapist Joe is named after Jay Renfroe's father and Betty Etiquette is named after his mother.) "Dr. Gold got it immediately," says Renfroe. "We were watching the very first date and at one point the woman's shoulders dropped and Gold said, 'Stop the tape. Date's over.' And he was right." At least once in every date, Therapist Joe makes an appearance to offer some pearl of wisdom on the dynamic of the date.

Once the pilot was completed, Gold Coast pitched the idea to several companies. Rysher nearly bought it but the company was in the process of being sold to Paramount, so the deal was never completed. Then Polygram Entertainment under Bob Sanitsky stepped up to the plate, bought the idea, and financed the pilot. From the beginning, *Blind Date* was planned as a "strip show"— that is, a program that airs every day of the week. Therefore, it was sold into syndication as opposed to airing on a network. Under the sales leadership of Matt Cooperstein, *Blind Date* was soon sold to markets in 85 percent of the country. But before the show could air, trouble struck once again. Polygram was sold to Universal. Luckily, the new parent company was also enthusiastic about *Blind Date*. Universal decided to stay with the show, in association with Gold Coast Television Entertainment, and launched the series.

Blind Date made its television debut in October, 1999. In no time flat, the show became a genuine phenomenon, moving swiftly from unknown quantity to guilty pleasure to time-slot-winning hit. Critics seemed to want to hate it (*Rolling Stone* said at one point, "*Blind Date* is the most toe-curlingly painful half-hour on television.") but most just couldn't bring themselves to (*Rolling Stone* wrote a year later, "Go ahead and call it just a shallow syndicated dating show. I call it a deeply meaningful part of my social life."). In fact, most critics just loved it. *Elle* magazine admitted that the show is "undeniably hilarious."

And even *Time* magazine called *Blind Date* "underrated," adding, "Not only is the writing on this reality show inspired, but repeated exposure should lower the divorce rate."

So, what is *Blind Date* exactly? Despite what *Time* magazine said, it isn't actually a reality show, even though it does have some elements in common with shows like *Survivor* and *Big Brother.* It also isn't a documentary on cultural anthropology, although citizens of the future will certainly be able to learn a lot about social interaction in our time by watching the hundreds of singles who have appeared on *Blind Date* act and interact. And it isn't exactly a comedy show, although laugh for laugh it is the equal of some of the funniest programs on television.

Executive producer David Garfinkle believes that it's the combination of elements that makes the show unique. "It's hysterically funny—that's what keeps people coming back," he says. "But the relationship aspect is what grabs people's imaginations, that's what viewers really relate to. You know, we're all experts on relationships—we never hesitate to give our friends advice. That's what the show is—a running commentary on other people's dates."

In short, *Blind Date* is simply *Blind Date.* It is, as host Roger Lodge has put it, "the show that lets you experience the fun of a blind date without the fear of rejection" or "the show that allows you to witness all of the danger of a blind date from the comfort and safety of your own home."

Each half-hour episode is composed of two blind dates. Each couple has been followed around by a *Blind Date* camera crew for a long, usually very eventful, date that typically lasts from eight to ten hours. Why so long? Executive producer and co-creator Thomas Klein says, "We try to create an environment where they start to get unaware of the camera . . . after the first hour, they forget the camera is there." And, once the couple has forgotten that the camera is there, they will start to act naturally and behave exactly as if they were on a "real" blind date.

Once the date has been committed to videotape, it's edited down to approximately six minutes, enough time to give the essence of the couple's story together. Then music, captions, sarcastic asides, thought bubbles, and psychological insight from Therapist Joe are added to lend humor—and sometimes horror—to the finished product. All of these additions take *Blind*

Date out of the realm of the reality show since, obviously, the thought bubbles are invented by the show's producers and the captions can change what really happened into something different—and something funnier.

"Our show is like talk-back TV," says executive producer David Garfinkle. "We just write what you'd be yelling at home."

Still, millions of viewers find *Blind Date* to be something more than just a comedy. It is also a voyeuristic window into the first moments of relationships that start out filled with promise and sometimes end up in emotional shambles. And, for those who are just entering the terrifying world of dating, the show is an excellent school on what you should—and shouldn't—do on a date.

For example, young women can watch a man on *Blind Date* woo and sweet-talk his date, saying all the right things, then go to the bathroom where he makes a cell phone call to a pal: "Dude, this woman is smokin'! Tits like you wouldn't believe!" When he comes back and starts telling her about his favorite book, *The Little Prince* (why? because it's about innocence), every woman watching has just a little better idea of how far some men will go to close the deal.

And men, watching a woman viciously attack her date verbally because he's "only" a supermarket manager ("Tomorrow, I'll wake up to my beautiful life and you'll still be you!") might gather a clue about what women really want. Which is, apparently, not supermarket managers.

But the dates that do work out are just as instructional in their way. Some couples on *Blind Date* talk to each other honestly, listen to each other completely, and make each other comfortable. Even those couples don't always end up getting a real romance out of the situation, but at least they made their date a pleasant event, and both of them were left with good memories—and that's a pretty good lesson to take away from *Blind Date*.

But there's no denying that the show has become so incredibly popular not for the love connections, but for the meltdowns, the dates from hell, and, of course, the frequent trips to the Jacuzzi. Sex and (emotional) violence is a big part of the show's appeal. Not that viewers want to go through an experience like that themselves, but they love the fact that they can watch from a safe distance and say, "Better you than me, pal." Some of the worst of the worst are discussed elsewhere in this book, from the screaming match on the sidewalk ("You zit-prone woman!" "Shut up, razor-bump ass!") to the abrupt termination of the date at about the halfway point ("Why are you doing this?" "I'm not. I'm outta here!"). But reading about them is not nearly as funny—or as gut-wrenching—as seeing them play out on the screen.

Because the company that produces *Blind Date* is located in Southern California, the great majority of the dates have taken place in and around Los Angeles. But the show continues to travel farther and farther afield—there have been special *Blind Date* weeks in Chicago, Toronto, Atlanta, Miami, Las Vegas, New York, and San Francisco. The producers intend to continue traveling to other cities across the country—in fact, plans are in place to take *Blind Date* to great locations around the world.

Actually, the show is already familiar to other parts of the planet. There is a German version of the show called *Blind Date* and one in the Netherlands entitled *Blind Match*. And there are soon to be foreign versions of *Blind Date* popping up in several other nations around the globe. And why not? The blind date is pretty much a universal concept. Except in some countries it's called "arranged marriage." Which isn't nearly as funny, you have to admit.

One measure of *Blind Date*'s success is the fact that so many parodies of it have begun to spring up on other shows. Hit television series like *Sabrina, the Teenage Witch* and *The Parkers* have done *Blind Date*–style episodes—and Roger Lodge even appeared on both programs in his role as host. MTV's *Andy Dick Show* and Fox Television's *Mad TV* have also done *Blind Date* spoofs. The Internet got into the act, too. *Blind Datrix,* a mixture of *Blind Date* and *The Matrix,* debuted on Ifilm.com early in 2001. And even comedy legend Steve Martin produced a short film as a parody of *Blind Date* in which he plays a man whose blind date is Claudia Schiffer.

As funny as each of those spoofs was, none of them could match the outrageousness and unpredictability of the best episodes of *Blind Date.* On nearly every show, the couples say or do things that come completely out of left field. They say things that a writer wouldn't come up with ("See, I'm looking for King Kong and I want to be the little girl in his palm. But now because I've had one drink, *I'm* King Kong and you're the little girl!" or "Is sushi Japanese?" "I don't know, it's some kind of –nese. Who cares?").

And situations arise that would be pretty hard to invent (like when one self-involved young lady tried on a sexy outfit and became completely transfixed by her reflection in the mirror, just murmuring "Oh my god . . ." over and over. Later, she and her date went dancing, but she soon asked him to sit down and she danced with herself, staring into a full-length mirror).

And sometimes, there is a scene of such dramatic perfection that it almost seems scripted—but it's not. Like the amateur magician who was boring his date to tears with his card tricks. She picked up a single die and said, "If I roll a six, can we get out of here?" He nodded.

She rolled a six. She stood up and said, "Now, *that's* magic!"

The dates on *Blind Date* certainly aren't always magic. But there's always something that is hilarious or dreadful, that makes you laugh or cringe. Or some interchange which makes some little comment on the human condition. Although best known for its disasters, *Blind Date* is essentially an optimistic show, always starting out with the hope that two people will find love. And it's kind of inspiring, too, watching just how much blood, sweat, and tears people are willing to wade through in order to meet someone special or, perhaps, to start a relationship that can last a lifetime.

The overriding tone of the average *Blind Date* episode is more likely to be bitter than sweet, but on reflection, the whole notion of the show can be kind of heartwarming. We all want love. And we're willing to do almost anything to find it. Even if it means risking ridicule on a national scale, as sometimes—heck, most of the time—happens on *Blind Date.*

This book is a kind of *Blind Date* companion. It will take you behind the scenes to show you just how the episodes are put together, and introduce you to some of the major *Blind Date* players, from Roger Lodge to Therapist Joe. And, by sharing good and bad examples from the show, this book can also serve as a kind of dating guide. The daters on the show can sometimes give you a great opening line or a smooth move. But more often, they're terrific illustrations of what you *don't* want to do on a blind date. Read about the "Dates from Hell" or the "*Blind Date* Meltdowns" and just try to do the opposite of what those people did and you should be in pretty good shape.

But really, no book can fully prepare you for the mean streets of romance. All you can do is get out there and learn how to travel along them in your own way. The best advice is still . . .

Be yourself.

And if you can't be yourself, be someone rich.

Dating Do's and Don'ts . . . Blind Date-Style

DO . . . bring a quarter, or, in some metropolitan areas, thirty-five cents, to make an emergency escape call. Or a cell phone. Or walkie-talkies.

DON'T . . . use the cell phone to call other friends while on your blind date.

DO . . . wear underwear.

DON'T . . . wear it on the outside of your clothing.

DO . . . read the newspaper the day of your date to make sure you're up on current events.

DON'T . . . regale your date with the recent adventures of "Funky Winkerbeam."

DO . . . have confidence and smile.

DON'T . . . grin like a maniac, stroke your date's hair and say, "um . . . purty hair . . ."

DO . . . bring breath mints.

DON'T . . . bring beef jerky.

DO . . . talk about a variety of subjects.

DON'T . . . keep bringing the conversation back to the time you traveled with a freak show.

DO . . . pay attention to the signals.

DON'T . . . lick your date's nose without being invited to.

DO . . . be honest.

DON'T . . . be *too* honest.

DO . . . meet your date at the venue rather than at home.

DON'T . . . forget where you told your date to meet you.

DO . . . share a soothing beverage.

DON'T . . . get blitzed.

1

DO . . . tell interesting stories about your past.

DON'T . . . tell bitter and embarrassing stories about your ex.

DO . . . have great conversation at dinner.

DON'T . . . talk with your mouth full. Or, about your mouth being full.

DO . . . order interesting appetizers.

DON'T . . . order anything with raw onions or garlic.

DO . . . show interest in your date's stories.

DON'T . . . doze off in the middle of one.

DO . . . ask interested questions about your date's job.

DON'T . . . ask how much your date earns.

Dating has changed a lot over the years. In the fifties, a keen date would be nothing more than a soda pop at the local soda shop, a hand-in-hand walk through the small town square and, perhaps, sex in the bushes. In the sixties, you might "groove" to the other-worldly sounds of Jimi Hendrix or Dinah Shore and just allow your inner oneness to connect with someone else's inner otherness and while your spiritual beings were astroplaning, your physical bodies could go bomb the post office.

In the seventies and eighties, as far as I can tell, people didn't date. But starting in 1999, when *Blind Date* went on the air, the practice came back into fashion—with a vengeance!

But by then, times had changed. For one thing, it wasn't the fifties or sixties anymore, except possibly in Mississippi. The dating scene of the New Millennium is a whole new futuristic world of cyberspace, singles bars, and, of course, deadly robots bent on world domination.

One of the things that changed is the life expectancy of a single person. According to some book I checked, people are remaining single longer than ever before in history, except possibly in prehistoric times when there were no justices of the peace. In the period just around World War II, for example, people would often be married by the age of twelve and dead by the time they got to Omaha Beach. Whereas in 2001, some people don't even bother to get married at all. And not just celebrities, but boring ordinary people, too. Statistics say that something like 75 percent of women age 20–24 and 80 percent of men of the same age have never been married. And some of them aren't likely to be. Statistics also claim that over 4 percent of adults have really big, ugly knees, but that isn't really relevant to this topic.

What does all this mean? It means that the dating scene is more competitive than ever before. And that more people are looking at dating as just a fun way to spend some free time as opposed to a way to select a life mate.

Just as there are more single people out there, so are there more busy people. Even finding the time to go on dates to find Mr./Ms./Other Right is virtually impossible, except for the jobless who are usually too depressed to date.

The dating pool, like a roiling tank of lawyers, is a place of such frenzied ferocity, in fact, that it might seem way too scary to dive into it, especially if you ate less than half an hour before going in. That's why we have complied this helpful list of do's and don'ts, *Blind Date*–style. We hope that by observing, step by step, what many of the show's couples have gone through, you can map out a plan of your own. After all, these people were on television which, by definition, means that they know more than you.

On the following pages, you will learn techniques for greeting your date; engaging in entertaining and enlightening conversation while driving to your first location; finding amusing and sometimes exhausting activities; enjoying a conversation at dinner, preferably without slurping; intimate conversation; and what to do, in addition to puckering, when it comes time for the goodnight kiss.

These rules don't apply only to blind dates. They should work— or not—for any one-on-one dating situation. And, our lawyers want to add, there are no guarantees attached. Maybe what got one couple to the hot tub will land you alone in a shower stall with nothing to comfort you but soap-on-a-rope. Not our fault. Don't blame us. The dating world is a landscape fraught, if that's the word I'm looking for, with danger, intrigue, and way too much coffee. The whole experience can be a little nerve-wracking. Heck, it can be downright terrifying. But you have to admit, it beats the alternative.

♥♥♥♥♥♥♥♥♥♥♥♥♥   ♥♥♥♥♥♥♥♥♥♥♥♥♥

Meet and Greet

DO . . . greet your date with a cheery smile.

DON'T . . . mutter darkly to yourself and lick your lips.

DO . . . introduce yourself with a fun fact.

DON'T . . . immediately describe in detail that hard-to-heal festering sore on the back of your knee.

DO . . . offer a gift of flowers or candy.

DON'T . . . try to pass off your old parking tickets as "Novelty Love Cards."

DO . . . share some exciting ideas of where you might go on your date.

DON'T . . . suggest any activity that takes place in your crawlspace.

It is often said by those who say such things, "You never get a second chance to make a good first impression." Although incredible advances in scientific research into the space-time continuum may one day prove this to be false, for the time being, this is a good thing to remember on a date. A blind date is something like a job interview—if you don't put your best foot forward at the beginning, there won't be any kind of payoff at the end, to say nothing of worker's benefits.

Of course, it's up to you to decide exactly which foot is your best. But it's always preferable to do a little preparation for that first moment when your date opens the door and drinks you in with his or her eyes.

Let's begin with the traditional favorite first date gift: flowers.

There are very few of us who wouldn't benefit from a little more color and beauty and from a more pleasant aroma. Of course, there are ways to accomplish these things over the long haul, but for a short-term result, flowers will help a great deal. As the poet Park Benjamin wrote, "Flowers are Love's truest language." But flowers also help you pave the road to love—they're the foundation of the good first impression. Sure, flowers are a cliché. But like other clichés—like, oh, "it ain't so much the heat as the humidity," for instance—they also ring pretty darn true. And if you have a face that's reminiscent of some of Earth's lower life forms or a figure that might serve as a tire advertisement, flowers can provide a nifty, if temporary, bit of camouflage.

There is an almost infinite variety of flowers and ways you can present them, and since you're making that all-important first impression, it would behoove you to give that presentation some serious thought. The lucky singles who have appeared on *Blind Date* have tried several variations on the floral theme—with varying degrees of success. If you find a technique that seems suitable for you, it might be a good idea to cross-reference the couple who used it elsewhere in this book. If they also show up in the "Dates From Hell" listings, you might want to go another way. But if they end up in the "Love Connections" or among the "Sexiest" dates, then maybe their first impression did its work.

Rob made a little treasure hunt out of his gift of flowers. When Constance came to his door, he led her to a huge display of teddy bears and gave her one. Then he read a little poem that directed her to another teddy bear—behind which was a bouquet. It took her forever to find the correct bear—even though its name was both in the poem and sewn in large letters across its stomach—but she was very pleased by the flowers nonetheless.

And so were the recipients of lovely bouquets of flowers in the dates of Vanessa and Jay, Kevin and Tania, Laura and Michael, Alyssa and Cameron, Jennifer and Tony, Heather and J.C., Jennifer and Keith, and Cheri and Brian, and many others. However, Shawn apparently misread the directions in the manual of love and brought Sarah . . . flour. Get it? He's a kidder.

Some people, finding an entire bouquet of flowers too ostentatious or expensive, choose the simpler alternative of presenting their dates with a single rosebud. This is the way Neils introduced himself to Elissa and the offering Jason made to Trish. And, turnabout being fair play, Kristen brought just one rose when she met her date, Matt.

Eric, being of a thrifty nature, actually picked flowers in Kelly's yard as they were walking to the car. It's probably never a good idea to present your date with weeds in the first moments after you've met. But a gift of flowers can sometimes bring something unexpected. Yulia was so pleased with the flowers that Jason gave her that she shared something personal with him right away—she showed him the fetish cage that stands ominously in her living room. And the memory of that dark iron contraption continued to fascinate him for the remainder of the evening.

Of course, a more imaginative dater can think of another gift besides flowers, or flour—one that will tell your date a little something about yourself. Sometimes, though, that gift can tell your date something about you that you didn't intend, as when Rockabilly Joe presented his date Olivia with two ugly kewpie dolls, or when Pete presented Charlene with, for some reason, a gift-wrapped can of Spam; at the end of the date, possibly inspired by his relentless jokes and even more relentless sweating, the can of Spam ended up in Charlene's garbage. That was very sad, as a more responsible place would have been the recycling bin.

El gave a T-shirt to Correnna. Maybe that could be construed as a romantic gift—until you noticed that the T-shirt bore the name of El's company. And that he urged her to put it on immediately and wear it throughout the date. He never actually asked her to make sure the logo was always pointed toward the *Blind Date* cameras. But it was implied. Once she put it on and they were driving along to their first activity, El said brightly, "I really appreciate it when a woman is well dressed."

In Atlanta, Jason was less commercial and more to the point when he offered Carmelle flowers and a book of erotic black poetry. However, since it turned out that Carmelle was celibate, with no intention of changing her status, the little volume of verse wasn't quite as effective as it might otherwise have been.

Kathleen, perhaps having heard that the way to a man's heart is through his stomach, offered Mark a batch of homemade cookies.

Kevin decided to make his first impression both sophisticated and childish. He galloped up to Nancy's house on a stick horse, holding a bottle of champagne. She responded, "You're such a nut!" which was, apparently, precisely what Kevin wanted to hear. And then she added hopefully, "Are you a stallion?" which is probably just what he didn't want to hear. But actually, these two hit it off very well and Nancy later admitted the horse had been "an awesome gift."

Timothy was not quite as romantic-minded as Jason nor as imaginative as Kevin; he brought his date Deana a Gators hat. But Vinny started things off on a hopeful note when he offered Angel a homemade fortune cookie with a message reading, "You will have fun with a redhead." The cookie was good, but the fortune turned out to be faulty. These two pretty much hated each other from the word go.

And Matt apparently wanted to leave Jessica a gift of a, well, different nature. As soon as he got to her door, he asked to use her bathroom.

Of course, there is a school of thought that avoids the idea of gift-giving altogether, choosing to start the date with a hearty laugh. For some reason, on *Blind Date,* this almost always manifests itself in that most hallowed of comedy props: fake teeth. When Christine met Steven she had her front teeth blacked out. He said, with a not altogether delighted tone in his voice, "Oh, a comedian."

Kevin wore a huge fake afro when he introduced himself to Gigi. And Chris put in huge false teeth, messed up his hair, and introduced himself to Renae as if he were a deranged hillbilly. At first sight, she said, "Oh my god," and went running down the hall. After Chris reverted to his everyday appearance, Renae was extremely relieved. She said, "You scared me."

And fake teeth proved to be the introduction prop of choice for Katelin and Mark, Angel and Aaron, Rachel and Jeff, and Aaron and Nina. At least that last date ended up in the Jacuzzi, so maybe it was one of those cases where the fake teeth really did work.

When Shari came to Kyle's door, he pretended not to be himself. Yes, it's comedy, folks! And you can see where their date wound up by checking out "Dates From Hell!" on page 80.

Some people find that they want to start things off by introducing their blind date to family, friends, or pets. This can work out well if it's important to show your new friend what a stable and sociable person you are. If, however, you introduce him or her to each of your thirty-eight cats, you might not be getting things started on the right foot.

When Melinda came to Adam's door, he introduced her to a roomful of his friends. She said, "It's like *Melrose Place* in here." When Janice met Denver she introduced him to her entire family—all women. Leland apparently wanted Marciela to know just what kind of a party guy he was, so he arranged for her to pick him up at his frat house, where his brothers hooted and hollered like, well, frat guys. And Jackie also lived in a frat house—the only female in a house with thirteen men. Todd was introduced around and seemed a little intimidated by the situation. And, as it turned out, the way they got along on the date pretty much assured that he was not going to become roomie number fourteen.

Christina, a single mom, also introduced D.P. to her entire family, including her baby daughter. This might have been a touching moment of bonding and familial warmth, except that D.P. had chosen to wear a "Who's Your Daddy?" T-shirt.

But, of course, there's family and there's family. For many single folk in the big city, pets are just like members of the family except that they are marginally more likely to drink out of the toilet. Jesselynn wanted Adam to meet her little Chihuahua and complained that she wanted to bring him along on the date. However, it didn't look like it was going to work out. Adam was, understandably, crushed.

But Misty did indeed bring her dog Tucker along on her date with Jerry. In fact, the dog became a vital part of the date's activities. They took him to get a bath, then surprised him with a treat from the doggie bakery. Misty told Jerry, "I like dogs more than I like people," which he had no trouble believing. The trouble was, Jerry soon fell under Tucker's spell as well. By the end of the date

Misty was saying, "I think you like the dog better than you like me." And that seemed to be pretty accurate.

Theresa also brought her dog along on her date with Dillon, to no better results. And Joe introduced Maura to his three dalmatians, which he called "my kids." They took the kids along for part of the date, romping with them in the dog park. And when Stefanie met Patrick, her dogs escaped from her apartment. He dutifully helped her round them up. Which should have bought him some brownie points for a few minutes later when he neglected to open her car door for her—but she never forgave him for his horrible, unspeakable rudeness.

And Christy introduced Robert to pets that could actually talk back—her macaws.

The first visual impression is important, of course, but the first conversational exchange also helps set the tone for the rest of the date. For instance, Peter's first words to Alana were, "Long time no see." She had to agree.

In those opening moments, it's best to dwell on something positive. When Domenica met Paul she summoned up the most sincere compliment she could think of at the moment: "I'm glad you don't have big ears. I hate big ears."

In the car, Karolyn admitted that this was her first blind date ever. Scott gallantly replied, "Oh my god, you must be desperate!" which is a good clue as to why the date ended with a weak salute and a tepid handshake.

Brian took one look at Sharyon and said the words that every woman longs to hear: "At least you're cute."

And it's always good to be able to return a compliment graciously. When David met Elizabeth, Miss Toronto, he said with obvious relief, "You're cute, I'm happy." She was offended by this and replied—and she wasn't kidding—"Can I say you're not cute? I'm not happy."

Not that your first words have to be compliments or idle pleasantries. In a scene that seemed kind of appropriate, since the date took place in New York City, Joe broke the ice with Diana by informing her that someone had just died in her apartment building.

Courtesy is always a plus, as well. And if your date isn't courteous, you might consider busting him or her on it immediately. Really. You'll find that almost everyone appreciates being corrected or criticized by a virtual stranger. When Philip neglected to open the car door for Rocki, she let him know right away that she wasn't used to being treated in this brutal manner: "I'm not a modern day girl. Chivalry!" Needless to say, that kind of warmth permeated the entire date.

However, of all the ways to make a good first impression, it would be hard to top the way Laurie chose to introduce herself to Mike. Walking to his door, she unbuttoned her shirt completely so that his first view of her included what guys generally regard as a sight for sore eyes. Sure, it's probably not the way your parents met, but it really seemed to do the trick. These two got along *very* well for the rest of their date. *Very* well indeed.

But when all is said and done, the most important thing is to start out your date with a sense of optimism. As John and Pamela were leaving her apartment building, they passed two women in the hallway. John said to them, "Wish me luck, ladies." One of the women asked, "Are you getting married?" John replied, "Well, maybe." As it turns out, John and Pamela didn't get married. But his statement wasn't really made out of turn. You might take many things along with you on your blind date, but the most important one is a sense of hope.

The First Conversation in the Car

DO . . . share school stories.

DON'T . . . tell your date how long you belonged to the cult.

DO . . . tell amusing childhood anecdotes.

DON'T . . . curl into a ball and moan, "Mommy . . . why do you hate me?"

DO . . . share a favorite joke.

DON'T . . . confide that you sometimes dream of bathing in the blood of the innocent.

DO . . . tell your date about your hopes and dreams.

DON'T . . . tell your date about that unfortunate incident under the bikers' clubhouse.

On *Blind Date*, and probably for the majority of dates in the so-called real world, a couple's first real conversation takes place while driving to the first activity. This is a terrific time to let your date know a little about yourself—but you should resist the temptation to get too confessional right off the bat. Those things have a way of coming back to haunt you later. And, you might want to avoid terrifying your date mere moments after you meet. At least, unless that's the kind of atmosphere you're going for.

Like the moment when Shelley told Joseph that her past boyfriends "are just evil. They need Jesus." Joseph said, "Uh-oh," and he meant it. He didn't have anything against Jesus, but he felt—correctly—that he had just gained a little insight into the way Shelley viewed all men. And it wasn't good. In trying to prove to her that he was different from the rest, he ended up toadying to Shelley for the rest of the evening—even letting her force him into buying her flowers.

Ian also handed over control of the date to Rebecca when he handed over the keys to the Expedition and let her drive. Rebecca said with a smile, "I'm in the driver's seat now!" But Ian's gesture actually made Rebecca like and respect him more; she recognized that he was treating her like a lady—just as any southern gentleman would do.

Alisha also took the wheel on her date with Craig. But he never gave up control of the date, bragging about his Porsche and engaging her in deep conversations about astrophysics, religion, and, of course, sex.

Amanda and Cary learned early on that they both come from almost the same part of Illinois. This common background put them immediately at ease with each other and soon they were making lots of Illinois jokes and cracking each other up. She also had a beauty queen title with which to wow him—it turned out that she had once been crowned "Miss Normal." Yeah, Normal is a town in Illinois, but after watching her on this date, you can't help wanting to crown her "Miss Normal" all over again. She was just a normal, lovely woman. And Cary obviously wanted to be "Mr. Normal" in the worst way.

Susan and Rico also had a lot to talk about. As soon as they started talking in the van, they were very surprised by just how much they had in common. They were both New York Italians, for starters, but it went far deeper than that. For one thing, they were definitely the first and only couple in the history of *Blind Date* who could and did quote Chaucer to each other. Or, possibly, even knew who Chaucer was.

Shay and Leon had something in common, too. In the car they found out they were both in the Marines. After they shared some funny anecdotes about life in the Corps, the sparks started flying and they knew they could be "Semper Fi" to each other—well, at least for the remainder of the date.

There are other subjects that don't bring people together as well, however. Griffin insulted Monika when he asked her if she had ever had plastic surgery or a breast enhancement. Since she was a model for *Perfect 10* magazine, she felt that this was the kind of question one just doesn't ask.

And as far as Jen was concerned, there are plenty of topics of conversation that one just doesn't introduce. It wasn't so bad when Jay told her how he likes to paint his toenails. But she definitely became more than a little uncomfortable when he began describing in some detail how he doesn't like toilet paper and prefers to use baby wipes on himself. Jen no doubt felt that his attention to hygiene was admirable, but ten minutes into the date may have been a little soon to begin sharing bathroom habits.

♥♥♥♥♥♥♥♥♥♥♥♥♥ ♥♥♥♥♥♥♥♥♥♥♥♥♥♥♥

The Blind Date Songbook

DO . . . write a poem that describes your date's physical beauty.
DON'T . . . write a poem that includes the word "Nantucket."
DO . . . try to capture your date's spiritual essence in song.
DON'T . . . honor your date with songs entitled "Knuckle Scraper" or "O, Those Bleeding Gums."

Guys:

DO . . . remember that all women everywhere love all men who play the guitar. There are no exceptions.
DON'T . . . forget to bring your guitar.

Gals:

DO . . . remember that men love women who can sing, and will try to manage their careers and then, after the woman has been used up and can no longer perform, will marry a younger woman and try to manage *her* career.
DON'T . . . date a guy like that.
DO . . . try to work your date's name into the lyrics of your song.
DON'T . . . do this if your date is named "Nantucket."
DO . . . try to show your sensitive side in your poem.
DON'T . . . write a verse about how you get creeped out by soap scum.

There are at least two distinctive *Blind Date* sounds. The first comes from the driving, guitar-based themes and incidental mu-

14

sic provided by the show's resident musical wizard Devin Powers. The second is provided by some of the daters themselves. Now and again, the singles on *Blind Date* find it useful to write poems to each other, or create songs out of thin air. Sometimes this works as a tool for promoting intimacy. And sometimes the song just makes every dog that hears it howl with anguish.

Here are a few of the musical and poetic masterpieces that have been created for *Blind Date,* as well as a *Behind the Music*–style look at how each work was created, and what kind of impact it had on the date.

Erica and John started their date by going to a local park and writing a poem for each other. John said the only rule was that they had to "keep it real." After they finished, Erica, for some reason, climbed up into a tree and read hers:

> Erica's poem:
>
> I am what I am
> Is it a woman or a man?
> Is it a dream or reality?
> I don't really know
> Where this point will go
> But hopefully it will land
> On the beach without no sand.
> That's impossible.

John was a little baffled by the "is it a woman or a man" line, and rightly so. However, his poem made it very clear that he was assuming that Erica was a woman.

> John's poem:
>
> I like your style
> And your West Coast flow
> But I keep thinking about
> How far this gon go.
> 'Cause you lookin' good

Wearin' all that blue
And I can't wait to get you home
To do that thing we all love to do.
And that's the end of my poem!

Now it was Erica's turn to be nonplussed. Seeing the blank look on her face, John laughed and said, "I kept it real!"

"That was *too* real," she said. "I think I should stay up in this tree and climb higher."

John's and Erica's poems didn't seem to form much of a bond between them. And, as it turned out, the verses weren't even the highlight of the date. That came later, when the two visited an amusement park and went through a haunted house together. Erica became genuinely terrified and ran screaming for safety. One of the great *Blind Date* moments.

In the end, John was interested in a second date, but Erica wasn't.

Rene and Devinna had a date that was filled with poetry and dancing—and lots of good chemistry. Devinna, 26, says that she's good on the dance floor but in real life she has her good and bad points. "I'm kinda stubborn. I'm spoiled. I have a big heart. When I feel comfortable with a man, I pretty much open up completely."

Rene, 23, is a poet who goes around saying things like, "The beauty of a rose can only be appreciated by someone who is patient at heart. Like a woman's heart." Huh? He also says this about himself, "I take my time with everything. One of the turnoffs is one of the fast beginners. I like the tease, the hunt. I like to get them ready so I can initiate and sensuate." Okay, there's no such word as "sensuate," but you get his drift.

Rene and Devinna met at his house, then went for a dance lesson. It turned out that they were both terrific dancers and kept up with each other step for step—always a good indication of compatibility.

Then, it was off to the family fun center where they raced go-karts. Rene was chivalrous and helped her into her car, and they made a bet. Rene said if he lost, he would have to rub her feet, which were sore from the dance lesson. If she lost, she would have to rub his back.

She won. One foot massage in the bank.

As they walked down the sidewalk, he made sure that he was walking on the outside. He said that in some countries, when a man and woman are walking together and she is on the outside, it means that the man is pimping her out. Devinna was amused by this information but didn't ask how Rene knew so much about it.

Over drinks, Rene decided to put the whole romance thing into high gear by reciting some of his poetry to Devinna. It went a little like this:

A Woman Sweet and Kind

A forest beauty is that I see
So sweet and innocent as lovely as thee
A touch from you I can only pray to feel
Because for that even an eagle will deal
So continue to walk with style and grace
Until once again I can touch your face

Devinna, obviously not a student of poetry, exclaimed, "Oh my god, that was nice!" and then added, "This is the best date I have ever been on."

On the ride home, she talked a lot about how compatible they were. She said, "We can see eye-to-eye. We are somewhat equally yoked."

Rene said, "I am having a great time." And to make sure that Devinna was having a great time, he then reminded her that he was a gentleman and he did lose a bet—and so he massaged her feet.

A love connection.

When Kim first met red-haired Canadian Scott, she didn't seem all that impressed. But his self-deprecating humor really appealed to her and eventually won her over. Did we say self-deprecating? Check out this song that Scott sang to her early in the date.

Chicks Don't Dig Me

Yeah yeah, chicks don't dig me
No no no no no chicks don't dig me

Every girl I meet just wants to be friends
As far as I'm concerned they're all lesbians
Maybe it's cause they think I'm gay
It's my apartment's pink, I didn't mean to paint
it that way

Yeah yeah chicks don't dig me
No no no no no chicks don't dig me

Maybe it's cause I got a massive head
No one takes you seriously when
Your pubic hair is red
Still I'd like to try to get a date
At my age a night of passion
Shouldn't mean I masturbate

Yeah yeah chicks don't dig me
No no no no no chicks don't dig me

"Chicks Don't Dig Me" is a song that might be a self-fulfilling prophecy, but as it turned out, Kim loved it. Even though they went on to a rather embarrassing body fat test and Scott revealed some less-than-flattering stories about his recent dating life, by the end of the evening, there was definitely one chick who dug him.

Soon after Laurie met George, she responded to something he said with, "Good. You're a smartass. I like that." He's also a special effects artist, a masseur and a whiz on the ukulele—which doesn't come up on *Blind Date* all that often.

Laurie and George shared aphrodisiac cocktails—and both claimed that the drinks worked—and found that they had all kinds of things in common, although Laurie's fascination with voodoo wasn't one of them. But at the end of the day, back at George's house, he sealed the deal with the special, made-to-order song which he sang, accompanying himself on the uke:

George's Ukulele Song

Come on Laurie give me a chance
I'm not trying to get in your pants
'Cause I knew from the very first glance
You were the one for me

What's the matter Laurie?
You look so irate
You took your chances
That's what you get when you
Go on a show called *Blind Date*

If the song was written to bring out positive results, the mission was successful. Laurie said, "No one's ever written a song for me before." And even as the final notes lingered in the air, George and Laurie were letting their lips communicate in a different way altogether.

Theirs was a major love connection. To paraphrase George's song, "That's what you (sometimes) get when you go on a show called *Blind Date*."

Sometimes the best songs in the "*Blind Date* Songbook" are completely off the cuff or, if you will, spur of the moment. Annie was a 26-year-old art student who wore her blonde hair in corn rows and could be measured by most reasonable standards as "a knockout." Bret might have been knocked out by her, but he was way too cool to show it. He's 30, an art director by trade and a harmonica player by avocation. Their date was pretty romantic, all in all. They drew each other's portraits, played a quick game of Ping-Pong, then enjoyed a little dinner with a lot of wine. Bret wasn't the most sensitive guy on Earth—he kept trying to put a flower in Annie's hair, and kept stabbing her with the thorns on the stem. Annie's dinner conversation consisted of small talk, personal family history, and about a dozen loud cries of "*OW!*"

Nevertheless, when they strolled down the street and he played her a little tune on the harmonica, all the *ows* seemed to be forgiven.

Later, in the backseat of the cab, Bret played again and urged her to make up a song. Which she did.

The Bret and Annie Blues

My baby left me
I don't know what to do

All I can say
Is boo hoo hoo hoo

Aw, he left me
Oh, man he left me!
Oh yeah!

Sadly enough, the song proved to be prophetic. Although they ended the date with clear intentions of seeing each other again, Bret never called Annie. "I thought he was cute," she said. "He was definitely my type and I was totally into him." Annie told *Blind Date* that she was hurt when he didn't call but she's over him now. Annie isn't one to sing the blues for long.

Martha also made up a song on the spot for her date, Michael. But for some reason he found the subject matter to be a little unsettling—even though he suggested the theme himself.

Martha is 26 and grew up all over the world—she's a military brat. Which gave her a lot in common with 28-year-old Michael, since he's a military man himself. On their date, they learned to ride a unicycle and took an African dance class. And, of course, they shared a lot about themselves through in-depth, personal conversation. Martha may have gotten just a tad *too* in-depth when she confided to Michael that she had once stalked a former boyfriend.

This revelation seems to have intimidated Michael a little— although he's a pretty tough guy to intimidate; in fact, at one point, he bench-pressed Martha, which is something *Blind Date* suggests saving until the second date.

At dinner, they started talking about her talent as a songwriter. "Give me a topic," she said, "and I'll write a song about it."

Michael suggested, "Do you have one about stalking?"

And, true to her word, she made one up:

> Martha's Stalking Song
>
> I see you there
> But you don't see me
> I see you there
> I'm watching you from a tree.
>
> I got a big old rifle
> Why can't you be with me?
> I see you there
> Watching you, sitting up in a tree.

At the conclusion of the song, there was a glint of fear in Michael's eyes. "It was very nice meeting you," he said. "Can I have my card back?"

It isn't entirely clear whether it was the song or some other factor, but the date slid slowly downhill after that. Michael and Martha went to the House of Blues where they danced to the music of Big Bad Voodoo Daddy. Unfortunately, Martha mostly danced by herself and Michael mostly danced with other women—definitely a blind date no-no.

There was no second date. And there have been no reported stalking incidents . . .

Venus and Darian learned a little about themselves through the art of poetry. For one thing, they learned just a little about their hopes and dreams. For another, they learned that they're lousy poets. But then, they probably knew that going in.

Venus is 22 years old and says that she loves to shop, talk, and "be me!" She describes herself as "extreme" and says the kind of guy she's looking for has a nice smile, a great body, and has to be easy to talk to. Sounds like she's describing Darian. He's 24 and calls himself an outgoing, childish professional who loves solving problems. He's looking for a woman who is also outgoing and childish . . . and he wants her to be creative.

Their first stop involved getting made over with Halloween makeup. Venus was transformed into a wolf. She thought she looked more like a bear, but no matter what she was, she liked turning into a beast. Darian got pointed ears, not unlike a particular *Star Trek* character. But unlike Venus, Darian was not particularly taken with his new look. Venus wasn't either; she told him that he looked like "a broke elf."

Still in makeup, they drove over to a park and tossed the football around. Then they sat down at a picnic table to write poetry about each other. And here's what they wrote:

Poems in the Park
by Darian and Venus

Venus:

I met this guy
On a blind date
I thought it would be great.
We went to a costume shop
And they made me look
Like a bear
But my date looks
Like a broke elf with no hair.

Darian:

This nice lady came through
When I saw her I was like, Cool!
Let's see what else we can
Get into.

Well, although their poems should have killed the date then and there, Darian and Venus kept going. Unfortunately, the more her wild side came out, the more conservative he got (like a mighty bear and a timid elf? Hmm?). They eventually worked their way over to a bar where they played an epic game of darts. The game had a special bet riding on it. If Venus lost, she would kiss Darian's cheek. If Darian lost, he would kiss her feet. Predictably enough, Darian lost and ended up on his knees, making out with her toes, which is all the action he was destined to get that night. Except that, gracious winner that she is, Venus gave him a kiss on the cheek after all.

In the end, Venus told *Blind Date* that Darian never had a chance—he just wasn't wild enough for her. Maybe it's true what they say: "Men are from Mars and Venus is from Venus."

Now, the era of the singing cowboys like Gene Autry and Roy Rogers is long over. But *Blind Date* brought it back very briefly on this date between Sharon and Jon. Sharon is a 27-year-old aerobics instructor from Long Beach, California, who calls herself outgoing, fun-loving, and sporty. Sharon is looking for a man who is fun, tender, and likes adventure. And she got one. Sharon was set up with Jonathan, 27, who describes himself as polite, intelligent, and outgoing. He is also a cowboy. No, he isn't from Texas or Wyoming or Montana. This cowboy was brought up on Long Island, New York, and currently lives in San Diego. And he's not exactly the John Wayne/Clint Eastwood kind of cowboy who rides and ropes and shoots and gets into brawls at the local saloon. No, Jon is the kind of cowboy who coordinates his outfits so that his wallet and hat and scarf match. And who makes sure his jeans have a nice crease.

But even though Jon lacks a certain credibility as a cowboy, that's the card he plays—and he plays it for everything he's got. He took Sharon horseback riding (and he had to ride with a helmet instead of his ten-gallon hat, which is always humiliating for a real cowpoke) and later took her on a horse-drawn carriage ride, except with different horses.

Sharon seemed to have fun without ever taking Jon very seriously, even when he told her that he had written a song especially for her. Taking out his guitar, which all cowboys like to keep handy, he sang for her.

Jon's Song

Well, all they'd tell me
Was her name was Sharon
My biggest question was
What I'd be wearin'

I first saw her
My jaw hit the floor, man
All my fantasies
Just walked through my door

Waited awhile for
This day to come along
Is she Mrs. Right or is she
Mrs. Wrong?

Either way, well
Things went fine
Will she say yes if
I ask her out another time?

(chorus)
I'm on a Blind Date
To figure things out
Put my best foot forward,
Show her what I'm all about

> On a Blind Date
> Between me and you
> I'll make your dreams come true.

Sharon responded positively with a "Woo! That was awesome! Very creative! I love it!" And she was too polite to mention that he even managed to discuss his wardrobe within the lyrics of the song, just as he constantly did in their conversation.

Ultimately, even with the serenade, Jon and Sharon ended up more like brother and sister than romantic partners. Apparently hoping for more cowboy thrills, *Blind Date* later set Jon up with a second chance—which turned out to be pretty much like this one, only with no song.

Dan also used a song to seduce Jillian—and with considerably more success than Jon had with Sharon. However, it must be admitted that his song, made up on the spot, isn't quite so well crafted as Jon's. In fact, it was only barely a song. Still, it seemed to do its job.

Dan isn't a songwriter, per se. This 25-year-old is a general contractor. He still lives with his parents and with his twin brother Nart (yes, Nart)—who has also been on *Blind Date*. Jillian is only 21 and characterizes herself as a "daddy's girl," which gave her something in common with Dan right off the bat.

From the moment Dan met Jillian (he called her "foxy" the first thing) he determined to lure her back to his bunk bed of sin, and pretty much everything he did or said on the date was dedicated to that general theme. He kept putting the moves on, relentlessly. She protested that he was too much of a "singles bar" kind of guy for her—she doesn't like the players. And every time he tried to kiss her, she ducked away.

But when he announced that he was going to seduce her with his guitar, the tide began to turn. Luckily, it turned out that he meant he would seduce her by *playing* his guitar. He began strumming away and improvising a song that sounded much like Lou Reed, recently awakened from a nap. It went something like this:

Dan's Song
(we presume the title is "Like Bees and Honey")

Tonight we'll stick together
Like bees and honey
Me and Jillian were
Chillin' on the beach
We're fallin', rollin'
Hope tonight we'll stick together
Like bees and honey
Like bees and honey
Like bees and honey
Like bees and honey
Like bees and honey
Like bees and honey
Like bees and honey
Like bees and honey
Like bees and honey
Like bees and honey
Like bees and honey

After that, apparently stunned by the depth and imagery of his lyrics, Jillian announced that she wanted the night to continue. They went back to his house and he promised to take her home in the morning. Guys, what has this taught us? Learn to play the guitar. Right now. Stop reading this and start strumming. Now. If "Like Bees and Honey" will work, almost anything will.

Xavier's rap didn't close the deal with Flame all by itself—but it sure helped. Actually, these two connected on just about every level there is. Flame is a 25-year-old clerical administrator from Los Angeles. She claims to have a way with words and describes herself as "a natural-born comedian." That means that the guy who hooks up with her should have a good sense of humor. And, at the very least, he should be creative when he's making puns on her name.

Her date, Xavier, is 30 years old and grew up in Oakland. He describes himself as "nonstop," "always on the go," and "living the hell out of life." Xavier is looking for a woman with long legs, nice hands, and a nice shape. And when he met Flame, he knew that she met every one of his qualifications. Plus, her name was Flame—that's just gotta be worth something.

Flame and Xavier had instant chemistry with each other. Xavier said and did all the right things to turn his date on. You might even say Flame was burnin' with desire, but that would be too easy. Their first activity was at a recording studio where she played the bongos (terribly) and Xavier improvised a romantic, free-styling rap just for her.

Xavier's Rap

The sound of rain against my window pane
Is mesmerizing to me
It's like those cold windy nights
When we made love past three
And we embraced, face to face,
Each and every night
And sweat from passion from the dusk
Until the morning light.
I waken to you and you waken to me
I'm feeling oh so happy
'cause it wasn't a dream
Now I see, 'cause if I risen
And your face wasn't there
It would have seemed as if
I was wakin' up straight to
A nightmare
This story thing
To the sound of the rain
I gotta have you right now, girl
I got to taste the Flame!

So what woman can resist a rap like that? Certainly not Flame. And expecially when Xavier followed it up with plenty more sweet talk. They ended the evening in a Jacuzzi, and this was one case where the couple was hotter than the hot tub. They made definite plans to see each other again and take things to the next level, whatever that means.

Eric's poem wasn't written especially for Kelly—and it wasn't particularly romantic or sexy. Not at all, in fact. But judging from all the kissing and sweet talk that followed on their date, the poem must have done its work.

Kelly is a 25-year-old hair stylist from Cypress, California, who describes herself as outgoing, fun to be with, and lovable. Her ideal mate has dark hair, has no body hair . . . and is able to play catch with her. We set her up with Eric, who has dark hair, at least. He's 32 years old and says that he's mystical, philosophical, and creative. He also likes to dot his I's with little stars, which should tell you more about him than any psychological profile ever could. He says that he's looking for a woman who is not only physically beautiful, but also secure and intelligent.

Eric started the date with a romantic gesture. As they were walking from her apartment building, he yanked a couple of flowers and weeds from the ground and offered them to her. She accepted the gift as graciously as if it weren't a huge, cheap insult.

Almost immediately he started talking about his poetry and, as they drove along, he recited one for her:

Eric's Poem

Love is a test of the
Emergency soul casting
System, brought to you
By the universe,
Sponsored by love . . .
If this had been an actual
Emergency, your heart
Would tell you what to do.

Kelly responded to this by smirking and saying, "Very clever." Eric made up more poems for Kelly at dinner and told her stories about his "bad boy" past. "I went to school," he said, "but I skipped all of the classes." At one point she seemed to be put out by his philosophical talk and Eric asked Kelly if she was mad.

"Why would I be mad?"

"Sometimes I say things that are like indigestion to some people."

Noting that there was a full moon, Eric massaged Kelly for a while, then kissed her. And kissed her and kissed her and kissed her. They kissed for a long time.

They kissed even more when they were saying goodnight and it looked like a certain second date. But, in the final analysis, neither was very sure what would happen in the future. Perhaps the Emergency Soul Casting System will give them a few hints.

Activities

DO . . . enjoy an activity with plenty of sunshine and fresh air.
DON'T . . . go anyplace where you will be exposed to toxic fumes.
DO . . . engage in healthy, lighthearted competition.
DON'T . . . play any game that involves unexploded land mines.
DO . . . go for an exhilarating drive in the countryside.
DON'T . . . allow your automobile to become your date's getaway car.
DO . . . come up with a creative project that you can work on together.
DON'T . . . plan the overthrow of any local government.

A normal date might consist of nothing more than dinner and a movie or perhaps a visit to a club for drinks and dancing. But couples who appear on *Blind Date* have a day and evening just chock-full of activities. Since they have just been chatting away in the van, the activities are a great way to have them interact in other, more physical ways, in order for them to get to know each other better and faster. When planning your own blind date, you might consider the things that the daters have done on the show. And you might look at those things that went horribly wrong and make a mental note to avoid them.

Actually, the activities on *Blind Date* have been just as varied and unique as the daters themselves. Some of them are great fun—parasailing, strip bungee, and body painting—while others are just peculiar; one couple actually learned how to dry-clean clothes. And it was a riveting few minutes of television, made even more so by the huge sweat stains in the woman's armpits.

Melinda and Adam played volleyball with a gaggle of teenage

girls—and they won! Then it was on to a rousing game of strip putt-putt. Nobody did a great deal of stripping, but they did go wading in the pool, or water hazard. She splashed him, playfully, so he picked her up and dunked her in the freezing water. Seemed a little mean.

Many couples on the show went to the gym together—of course, for young singles in Los Angeles, that's practically home away from home anyway. But Peter and Alana went to a boot camp workout on the beach. It was exhausting but they seemed to enjoy it. Alana said, "I always feel that I look my best when I'm hot and sweaty." Pamela and Kirk had a boot camp experience, too—but that one didn't turn out nearly as well. Kirk was completely out of shape and spent the entire session complaining, moaning in pain, crawling on the ground, or yelling at the instructors. For more details, you can read all about their date in the "Dates from Hell" section.

Caroline and Jason chose a slightly more interesting—but just as painful—dating activity. They went to get Caroline's navel pierced. And Dale apparently hoped to catch a glimpse of Joy's navel—and, presumably, much more—when he took her to a nudist colony as the first stop on their date. As it turned out, Joy refused to get into the spirit of the thing, although Dale stripped down immediately.

Besides, who needs nudity to get a little naughty? Certainly not Alisha and Craig. They went on a motorcycle ride which Alisha, at least, enjoyed very, very much. At one point she shouted, "Who needs a vibrator!" And Craig just revved the engine harder, to Alisha's delight. She told him, "This is the ultimate foreplay!" And, as things turned out, it was.

Now, this must have seemed like a good idea to somebody, but it sure didn't help the date along when DeNiece and Brian went to visit, of all things, a foot doctor. They both got pretty grossed out. DeNiece had already mentioned that she could never date a man if she thought his feet were ugly (odd, she never mentioned anything about character or personality) and she evidently found Brian to have unsuitable feet.

Their next activity was at a fantasy fair where they pretty much had fun while ignoring each other. In fact, at one point, for reasons of her own, DeNiece decided it would be funny to flash her breasts to everyone—except Brian. This happened repeatedly and, although everyone who witnessed these acts of full disclosure found them to be charming and compelling in the extreme, Brian just got more and more depressed as the evening wore on, and DeNiece wore next to nothing.

And speaking of wearing nothing, Shay got to know Leon much better than she anticipated when they went to an art class for a drawing lesson. Shay figured she would be sketching a basket of fruit or something but she learned differently when Leon came out in a robe, took it off, and announced that he was going to be her model.

Another favorite *Blind Date* activity is a visit to the lingerie store. After all, what better way is there to get to know your date than by ogling him or her all dolled up in a teddy or lacey thong? Antonietta and Corey went one better. After they modeled different styles of lingerie for each other, they stepped out to the side of a busy street and tried to stop traffic in their underwear. Unfortunately, because they were in Los Angeles at the time, nobody seemed to notice.

Some of the couples on *Blind Date* choose more wholesome, G-rated activities. Tracey and Jamal went to a bakery where they learned to make beautiful gift baskets. She was much better at it than he was, and the entire exercise allowed them to get playful with each other and start to connect on a personal level.

The same thing happened when Correnna and El went riding on a merry-go-round. Correnna rode sidesaddle and El spent the whole ride telling her how beautiful she was. And he meant it, too—especially since she was still wearing his company's T-shirt that he had urged her to put on at the beginning of the date.

Evelyn and Steve went on a date in Chicago. Now, no place on earth has better pizza than Chicago, so these two went to a restaurant and learned how to make some of that deep-dish pizza. Would have been a fun experience except for the fact that Steve kept loading on the sausage, even after Evelyn told him that she was a vegan. He didn't seem overly interested in this revelation. In fact, it didn't seem to sink in at all. Because later, when they went to dinner, he took her to a steak house . . . a steak house where the waiter brings huge slabs of raw meat to the table so you can choose just which one you like. Here's a tip: no matter what your activity is, you might want to pay attention when your date is revealing major lifestyle issues.

Blind Date's singles have gone flying in airplanes, helicopters, and balloons. They've explored the seas on yachts, submarines, and surfboards. They've painted pictures, washed cars, created sculptures, and cooked gourmet meals. They've played Ping-Pong, miniature golf, actual golf, basketball, football, volleyball, chess, checkers, and video games. They've sewn quilts, strung beads, visited museums, picked fruit, and gone on hayrides. But when it comes to the oddest *Blind Date* activity ever, the nod just might go to Kimberly and Brian. They went to . . . a Lamaze class. Now, before you ask, neither one of them "needed" to be there—they just went to see what it was like. But, if you look at it from another angle, maybe it isn't so strange. After all, people who spend so much time giving each other lingerie fashion shows or making out in the hot tub are probably going to find themselves at Lamaze class sooner or later—so why not just get it out of the way?

Dinner

DO . . . show your classy side by choosing the nicest restaurant you can afford.

DON'T . . . take your date to any place in which your order can be supersized.

DO . . . make things romantic by sharing a delicious appetizer.

DON'T . . . offer your date some of the sandwich you've been keeping in your pocket.

DO . . . remember that conversation is more important than food, so don't order something too messy or chewy to interfere with getting to know your date.

DON'T . . . eat soup with your fingers.

DO . . . offer a taste of your meal to your date—that's a romantic thing to do.

DON'T . . . quickly lick all of your food and yell, "Dibs!"

DO . . . allow the conversation to become more intimate.

DON'T . . . show your date a list of people you'd like to kill.

DO . . . share a glass of wine, and make a toast to your date.

DON'T . . . drink the wine directly from the bottle, or call out to the waiter, "Garçon! More hooch!"

Dinner is a crucial time on a blind date. You've already spent some time driving around and doing activities with your date. Your first conversations were all of the "getting to know you" kind and the activities may or may not have been conducive to talk about intimate feelings, hopes, and dreams.

So dinner is where it really starts to be a date. Now is the time to bring up some serious topics and find out just how much you and this stranger really have in common. And it's an excellent opportunity to check out your date's table manners and food choices. After all, if you're a vegetarian and your date slurps down a huge bloody steak—and chews with mouth open, to boot—then you've just received a pretty clear signal to get this thing over with and move on.

But if your conversation begins to point up things you have in common ("Wow, *I* like French fries, too!") then the walls of defensiveness can begin to come down, allowing the invaders of intimacy to leap over the moat and destroy the armies of self-consciousness, establishing a beachhead on the shores of personal chemistry. Oh yeah, and if your date uses really forced and tortured metaphors to get his or her point across, send 'em to a writing class.

Let us once again look to the fine example of *Blind Date* for subjects that make up good, revealing dinner conversation. And to get an idea of just what kinds of things you *shouldn't* say.

At dinner, Adam tried to get Melinda to talk about her wild side. She was willing to do so, but there was just one problem—she doesn't seem to have one. She's a Mormon, for one thing. She's been abstinent for five years, for another. Melinda told Adam that she used to have piercings but now she doesn't like to talk about it.

El asked Correnna why she's single—that's the kind of question that can backfire on you if your date feels at all sensitive about the topic. Luckily, Correnna didn't feel that way, but her answer was a little chilling, anyway. "Actually," she said, "I'm concentrating on myself." Well, that answer *would* seem chilling to someone else, but El feels exactly the same way. He told her that he has been concentrating on himself, too—or at least his lingerie business. And once he brought it up, he launched into a long, long commercial for his product. Keep this in mind: it's virtually never a good idea to use a blind date as a way to sell your companion custom-made underwear.

Maja and Romeo had a pleasant enough time during dinner. But when she stepped away from the table, Romeo hit on the hostess and complained that his date was fat. Of course, Maja never knew this—until she watched her *Blind Date* episode—so when she returned, they resumed dinner and had plenty of laughs while exchanging funny stories.

The chemistry between Brooke and Uriah had been pretty much nil from the get-go, but at dinner, things started looking more romantic. But not for Uriah. Brooke had said that she was looking for an all-American, blond, blue-eyed man—and she found one: the waiter. She slipped him her number and Uriah tried to take it like a man.

Joseph, learning early on that Shelly is a devout Christian, asked her how her religious beliefs affect her sex life. Shelly replied that she was now celibate, partly because the Bible told her so and partly because she was "played by some players." Shelley said, "If you share something with someone and it turns out they didn't love you, it really hurts." Joseph, hoping against hope to change her mind, replied, "Only for a little while." This was not the answer Shelley was looking for. She said, "I rebuke you in the name of Jesus!" Which is, you'll have to admit, kind of a conversation killer.

Barbara talked to Robert at some length about her religion,

too—she's a Messianic Believer, which means, to hear her tell it, that she believes in Jesus Christ but basically practices Judaism. Robert seemed to be listening to her but was clearly disappointed at the clear subtext: no nookie. Actually, that subtext became even clearer later at dinner. She leaned over and whispered to him that she is planning to get married in the next couple of weeks to a man whom she has known for several years. Robert took it well, but he couldn't help but wonder why such a nice religious woman as Barbara would so cruelly jerk him around like that. She had no explanation, except that she thought a blind date would be fun. And indeed it was—just not for Robert.

Brandi didn't say anything of a religious nature to Brad. Far from it—her stories were filled with sexual details that would make Hugh Hefner blush. Possibly the highlight—which, for understandable reasons, never actually aired on *Blind Date*—was when she told him that she had once won a blow job contest. Now, every guy wants his date to be a winner and Brad regarded this story with a mixture of apprehension and ecstasy.

All through the date, Joe joked with Roxanne about his desire to be a porn star. Roxanne, naturally enough, was appalled. She was even more appalled when he got right up from the table and started dancing for her, eventually ending up stark naked. As it turned out, Roxanne wasn't the only one who was appalled by this. The owner of the establishment wasted no time in kicking them out.

Now Joe might have wanted to be a porn star but Cressa actually made Vincent act like one—even after he leaned in to kiss her and she pulled away from him in disgust. Vincent bragged that he was excellent at giving oral sex, so she challenged him to prove it. And that's exactly what he did, right there at the dinner table (they were in a private room). Sadly for him, she wasn't all that impressed and refused to return the favor. But luckily for him, the entire incident was way too over the top ever to be shown on *Blind Date*—so at least he didn't have her disappointment broadcast from coast to coast.

Joy and Dale didn't do anything dirty at dinner, but they had a very sexual conversation. The only thing was, Joy never really knew it. Dale (remember, this is the guy who took her to a nudist colony for their first activity) took a special delight in befuddling Joy—which, truth be told, wasn't all that hard to do. When the subject turned briefly to music, Joy said, "I'm not musically gifted at all. I can't play any instruments, I can't sing . . ."

DALE: "Have you ever played the um . . . skin flute?"
JOY: "No. What is that?"
DALE: "It's actually, for girls it's a really fun instrument to play."
JOY: "Really . . ."
DALE: "Yeah, yeah, you got to try it."

And later, Dale regaled her with one of his outdoor adventures.

DALE: "I went out fishing one time and we were fishing for ah . . . bearded clam; have you ever heard of that?"
JOY: "Uh huh. But you don't really fish for them."
DALE: "Kind of. The bearded clam is elusive."
JOY: "Oh my god. The bearded clam is elusive."
DALE: "Yeah, you fish for it, I mean most guys I know . . . you could even use hot dogs."
JOY: "Get out."
DALE: "A hot dog is a good lure for bearded clam. So, what you do is you throw it out there and once you get a bite you nail it."
JOY: "Oh yeah . . . you just throw a hot dog out and the clams are all clomp clomp and they go for the hot dog?"
DALE: "Yes and you nail it."
JOY: "You nail it. Pow! Right."

The dinner conversation can also be an excellent opportunity to talk about standards. For example, when Scott asked Michelle if she would consider posing for *Playboy* she replied, "I wouldn't do a beaver shot." Then she asked if his fantasy was to "be with" two girls at the same time. "No," he lied.

Rosa and Troy also talked about sex at dinner, discussing the pros and cons of casual sex, one-night stands and booty calls. But Troy's chances at any of the above dropped dramatically when she uttered the most horrible sentence known to man: "I look at you as a brother, you know?"

Troy tried to salvage things with a suave, "Deep down inside I know you are longing for me." But she told him in no uncertain terms that sex was definitely out of the question. Trying once again—and you have to admit it's creative, though lame—Troy said, "I'm a human sexuality major." Rosa smirked and replied, "Well, you got an F." See? You should never give someone a straight line like that. It can never lead to anything good.

Dinner is also a time that the date can go south in a hurry. Tenesia and Baron had their entrées with nitpicking and quarreling on the side. She was pretty steamed by many of the things he said, but the capper came when Baron called her by another name. That's when she blew her top. She said, "You make me never want to go on a blind date again."

The Last Stop

DO . . . suggest a quiet café that you know about.

DON'T . . . go to any place that serves both Chinese food and doughnuts.

DO . . . get sexy and playful with each other, perhaps by dancing or playing a quiet game of billiards.

DON'T . . . let your date talk you into getting into the trunk of his or her car.

DO . . . discuss, over drinks, how well your date went.

DON'T . . . illustrate just how well your date went by flinging your drink in your date's face.

DO . . . let your date down gently if you're not interested in a second date.

DON'T . . . stick your finger down your throat and make gagging sounds.

DO . . . go for a moonlight walk on the beach or through a nice park.

DON'T . . . look for a place in a dark alley to sleep it off.

DO . . . let your date know if you're feeling romantic.

DON'T . . . do that with too much eye-rolling and saliva.

Depending on how well dinner went, the next stop can either be a chance to really seal the intimacy deal, or try to do a quick desperate patch-up for all the stupid things you said over dessert. After dinner spots can range from bars to ice cream stands, from coffee shops to dance clubs. And, of course, the Jacuzzi (but more about that below). But no matter where you go, this is pretty much the final stage of the date. Any bonding that hasn't yet occurred must happen now or not at all. Whether you're hoping that the date will end with both of you back at your place or simply the promise of a second date, it's now or never.

El chose to make an eleventh-hour play for a booty call when he and Correnna went to play a little water football. El, not known for his subtlety, asked, "Have you ever done it in a hotel swimming pool?" Correnna replied that she hadn't and made it clear that she wasn't about to start.

Melinda and Anthony ended up at a pool, too, and it didn't work out any better for them than for El and Correnna. Anthony was pretty much fed up with Melinda by this point of the evening and announced that he was going swimming, whether she came along or not. Then he simple got up and left. She followed him to the pool, where she watched glumly while he swam around, all alone. When she complained, he said, "Hey, if you want to go home, just say so." Melinda, clearly not used to being the one treated like dirt on a date, said quietly, "I want to go home."

Peter and Alana ended the evening over drinks, both puzzled why their date had been such a bust when they were both such friendly and attractive people. Peter said, "Like when I first saw you I thought you were really pretty and I thought this is really the kind of girl that I'd like to go out with. And you're really nice and easy to talk to. But I don't know what it is, we're just not connecting. Do you feel that?"

"Yeah," she said.

"I mean, I think we've both had a lot more exciting dates," Peter said, which pretty much closed the door on this one getting any more exciting than it did.

There were no such declarations of defeat for Rebecca and Ian, though. They wound things up by playing pool and then went off to do a little hot oil wrestling. Once there, they chickened out and ended up watching instead of participating. But, hey, watching can do the trick, too. Ian planted a big kiss on Rebecca and she ended the evening by asking for his number, which she got.

Andrew had spent much of his date with April babbling out his theories of the world, such as why traffic lights are the colors they are, and why are we so quick to categorize things like, say, corn chips. April actually entered into these conversations but she eventually talked him into doing something that she wanted—she got a lap dance at a strip club. While Andrew chatted up the waitresses and strippers, April got up on the stage and cut loose, twirling around the pole like a pro. Andrew was fine with it, apparently sensing that her aura was being cleansed through fantasy fulfillment.

Michelle and Scott also ended their date with lap dances. In fact, they both got lap dances at the same time. So did Rachel and Justin. She was the young woman completely obsessed with the writings of Sigmund Freud. She talked freely with Justin all through the date about her sexual fantasies, orgies, and how much she enjoys watching two men make love. She kept dropping broad hints that she would like Justin to sleep with another man while she watched, but he kept changing the subject. However, they both seemed to enjoy their lap dances at the strip club. After all this, Justin seemed pretty sure that a sleepover was pretty much a done deal, but when he tried to kiss her, she only gave him a friendly peck on the lips. Later, Rachel admitted that she had just been teasing him all night long. She also admitted that she sometimes fantasizes about digging up Freud's bones. Oh, come on—like *you've* never thought about it?

For Alisa and Craig, his-and-her lap dances would just be too dull and conventional. At a bar, they began challenging each other to do outrageous things. First, Alisha kissed Craig. Then, he dared her to find a woman in the bar and kiss her. She did so. Then Alisha dared Craig to kiss another man. And he did. Then Alisha kissed *that* guy. Then Alisha and Craig kissed each other some more. Lap dances, hah! Alisha and Craig knew where the real action was.

So did Brandi and Brad. After hearing about her "torture table" all night long, Brad eventually agreed to be tied to it (it's in her carport, by the way). Once there, she didn't really torture him, but the event led to a lot of kissing.

What You Didn't See

But Laura did torture Jason—at least a little. Laura, banker by day, dominatrix by night, talked about her S & M interests with

Jason throughout the date. She got Jason so intrigued they decided to go for a little "session" after dinner. It turned out that she actually had a torture dungeon in her basement. Virtually none of this sequence made it onto the aired version of *Blind Date*—but here's what happened. Laura, in a black vinyl miniskirt, cracked Jason on the rear with a paddle, a riding crop, and a whip. Laura then strapped Jason to a giant cross and began spanking him. After that, she blindfolded him, put a dog collar around his neck and tied him to her own torture table. And then Laura led Jason around by a leash and forced him to bark like a dog. And at the end of it all, they were both anxious to go on a second date.

F.Y.I. Laura's decor was in Better Homes & Dungeons

Sometimes *Blind Date*'s singles get set up for a second date—but not with the person they're on *this* date with. New York couple Alyssa and Stephen got along kind of like a brother and sister throughout their date. Alyssa thought he was too chunky and mild-mannered for her. But at least two other women didn't think so. At dinner, while Alyssa was sitting right there, a woman showed up and slipped Stephen her number at the table. That made Alyssa angry, even though she wasn't interested in Stephen herself. After dinner they headed to a festival where another woman offered to take Stephen for a tour while Alyssa wasn't around. So even though he didn't make the grade with Alyssa, Stephen did all right on his blind date.

But Peter sure didn't. His date with Beth wasn't going all that badly until he let her have a look at his "list," which he keeps on him at all times to remind him what he wants in a woman. The list is very lengthy, and Beth insisted on reading it. And when she did, the date was effectively over. Peter's list said that he demanded a woman with large breasts, a shaved pubic region and the willingness to chew tobacco. Beth was appalled, not only that Peter actually felt this way, but that he wrote it down and kept it with him at all times—*and* that he showed it to her. Perhaps Peter learned a painful but valuable lesson—there are certain things that you just don't put in writing.

But you don't have to put things in writing when you have the animal magnetism that Justin had with Dori. And "animal magnetism" is used here in its original sense: Justin was a hypnotist. It's very odd—they got along okay in the early stages of the date. But after Justin hypnotized Dori in the park, she began admitting that she was "stimulated" by him and told him she was thinking about sticking her tongue down his throat. As long as Justin never snaps his fingers and brings her out of her trance, these two should get along just fine.

Rob was having trouble figuring out why he and Dominga weren't getting along fine. After all, he was being his usual charming self and saying all the right things. But at the end of the evening, she came clean. Dominga admitted that she had another boyfriend and was contemplating moving to London to be with him. Rob, feeling (correctly) that he had been played by someone who never should have gone out with him, was ticked in the extreme. He began making fun of "London Boy" and then told her he wanted to call it a night. During the cab ride home, he told her in no uncertain terms what he thought of her. Then, to add insult to injury, he made a cell phone call to set up another date as soon as he could get rid of this one.

Hot Tubs

♥

DO . . . get into the Jacuzzi only if you and your date are thoroughly comfortable with each other.

DON'T . . . get into a Jacuzzi in which the water is a brackish gray.

DO . . . enjoy the tingly sensation of the bubbling water.

DON'T . . . manufacture your own bubbles.

DO . . . show your date that you appreciate the beauty of his or her body.

DON'T . . . hoot loudly and shout, "Man! Them's big 'uns!"

DO . . . become as sensuous in the hot tub as your date is willing to get.

DON'T . . . try to initiate a game of Marco Polo.

DO . . . try to determine if you and your date are on the same sexual wavelength.

DON'T . . . try to determine if you will fit into your date's swimsuit.

DO . . . get romantic by calling your date a pet name.

DON'T . . . bring any of your own pets into the Jacuzzi.

There have been many destinations for the singles who appear on *Blind Date*. They have visited museums and junkyards, sports stadiums and go-kart tracks, wallpaper stores and amusement parks. But there is one destination that is special. It's a place of hope, magic, and wonder, a mystical spot where dreams come true and all the troubles of the world burst like bubbles. It is a spot where everything is good and beautiful, the location that Shakespeare called "the steaming cauldron of delight" and the Dead Sea Scrolls referred to as "the pond that simmereth. It relaxeth but lo it breedeth wilde urgencies in the thong area." It is, of course, that most sacred and mystic of dating destinations—the Jacuzzi.

The hot tub has been a favorite of daters since whenever it was invented, which was probably a long time ago. Its warm, steamy comfort is the perfect atmosphere for a relaxing end-of-date tête-à-tête, if you'll pardon all those dashes. Certainly, *Blind Date* never lets too many suns set without sending a couple to splash around in one Jacuzzi or another. The couples expect it and the audience expects it.

But there is one common misconception about the Jacuzzi (well, two, if you count the one that says the water makes an excellent stock for soup)—and that is that the couples who go there are destined for a night of love. As *Blind Date* has proven time and again, a mere visit to the hot tub means nothing, except possibly higher ratings. If the couple isn't romantic going in, chances are they won't be romantic coming out. But, as the poet said, "Hope springs eternal when the water is bubbling and the bikinis are tiny and loosely tied."

Let's take a look at some of the many couples who took a dip in the Jacuzzi and see what effect, besides prune skin, it had on them.

Jennifer and Tony talked about very little on their date except her rigid physical fitness regimen, with which she was totally preoccupied. Things looked up briefly for Tony when she started talking about going crazy with tequila body shots. However, she was in training, so that was out of the question. But she did consent to demonstrate her sexy body shot using a virgin tequila shot—which means water. That opened the door to a little light making out, but Jennifer quickly shut Tony down again and went right back to talking about her workout regimen.

It seemed to Tony that he might be able to turn the tide in the hot tub—and there was indeed a little action of the romantic kind. They gave each other massages and did a little making out. But even the Jacuzzi couldn't warm up this date. These two couldn't have worked up a spark in a match factory.

Stacey and Aaron brought many more positive vibes to their hot tub experience. They had already thoroughly bonded on a nice "country-style" date that included making ice cream sundaes and then picking and munching on strawberries at a cute little farm way beyond the city limits. By the time they reached the Jacuzzi, love was in the air—and, apparently, in the water—for

Stacey and Aaron. They flirted and smooched and snuggled all night.

Cassy and Simeon's date was not nearly as innocent as Stacey and Aaron's. These two were all about sex from the start. It was the main topic of conversation all night. They discussed the fact that they are both exotic dancers and he even showed her a picture of himself in his "Black Stallion" costume—leather chaps and cowboy hat. She came right back at him with photos of her in a men's magazine and showed him snapshots of her and her friends doing naughty things in Las Vegas. Even when they went to get candy at a specialty story, they managed to make eating sweets look positively X-rated.

So when they wound up naked in the hot tub, nobody was particularly surprised. But *everybody* was surprised when, after making out pretty seriously at her place for a while, she sent him home, telling him to save it for the next date. When they were saying goodnight, Simeon felt that Cassy was trying to give him a "grandma" hug—and he would have none of it. He proceeded to pick her up, grab two large handfuls of behind and give her a big wet kiss.

Danita and Todd didn't have quite as sensuous a date before they got to the Jacuzzi, although things started to heat up at about dinnertime. That's when Danita started using her fart machine to make Todd think she had terrible gas. Once he realized that it was only a joke, the bonding began. They did a peanut butter body shot, then went for a drink at a beach bar, and finally headed for the hot tub. There was some serious necking going on in the Jacuzzi, but things got even steamier when Danita decided to go for a dip in the swimming pool—topless. Needless to say, Danita and Todd's date was a bona fide love connection.

And speaking of love connections . . . Jen and Jason also had it going on throughout the entire date. At dinner the conversation got interesting when they started talking about each other's sex lives. Jen told Jason that she has a perfectly healthy one—by herself! The kissing began at the dinner table and, after they did a little slow dancing at a bar with a beautiful romantic view, they decided it was time to head for the hot tub. All that kissing at dinner turned out to be just a practice run—in the Jacuzzi, they indulged in the real thing.

So real, in fact, that it continued back at Jen's place. So real, in fact, that the *Blind Date* crew left a long time before Jen and Jason did, if you get the drift.

Sadly, Amy and Shawn didn't get along half as well as that. Shawn was smart enough to know that Amy had no interest in him. But Amy wasn't smart enough for Shawn. At dinner, things came to a screeching halt when Shawn, an avid reader, asked Amy what books she liked. She replied, somewhat proudly, that she had never read one. Shawn was then faced with the conflict that has haunted men and women throughout the ages—should he continue to put up with her just in hopes of having sex?

Unfortunately, the decision was soon made for him. At the Jacuzzi, Amy crawled to the opposite side to get away from him. He got the hint. The hot tub was a very cold place that night.

The hot tub didn't lead to romance for Tami and Brad either, but Brad wasn't complaining. For the first half of the date, Tami, a bikini model, seemed a little nervous and reserved. Brad's challenge was to figure out how to break down the wall that she had erected around herself—and he finally did. At dinner, he made a deal with her that if he allowed her to shave off his goatee, she would, in turn, try on lingerie for him and join him in the Jacuzzi. She agreed. They went off to Hustler Hollywood, where Brad learned precisely why Tami is a well-paid lingerie model. Then it was on to the hot tub, where Tami relieved herself of her outer garments once again. Wearing a teeny weeny green bikini, she relieved Brad of his facial hair. The whole thing didn't lead on to more dates or a big romance between them. But Brad would always treasure the memory of one close shave.

Nina and Aaron were just a little more into each other when they made their trek to the hot tub. They kissed each other—and even kissed each other's *feet*—and enjoyed giving each other a vigorous back massage. At one point, the massaging became so vigorous, that Nina's nipple made an unscheduled appearance.

Aaron wasn't frazzled by the sight. He said calmly, "It's all right—she just wanted to come out and check a brother out." And, judging from the way they acted on the way home, the brother must have checked out just fine.

The same couldn't be said, however, for Drew on his date with Christina. He was not the most thrilling guy who ever lived—and he seemed determined to miss every signal that Christina sent his way. She kept hinting about her out-of-control wild side—in fact, she practically laid it out before him and commanded, "Bring this out." But he didn't. He didn't even try. Christina mentioned to Drew that she had done some nude modeling for a men's magazine. She told him that she was an exhibitionist. She said that she loved to go party at Lake Havasu. She said her ultimate fantasy was to be a centerfold for *Playboy*. Drew didn't pick up on any of it.

Even in the Jacuzzi, Christina, made it perfectly clear that she wouldn't at all mind doing a little nude hot-tubbing. She put on a very sexy bathing suit and gave Drew a little show, to which he had almost no response. If there were a law against ineffectual use of a hot tub, Drew would be liable for a record-breaking fine.

Now Jerry wasn't that much more into his date with Kelly than Drew had been with Christina, but Jerry still made the most of what he had to work with. Jerry's a new arrival in this country from Great Britain. He's a wild bloke who talks a mile a minute in an accent that is not always easy for the American ear to decipher. Still, he knows how to have a good time. So does Kelly. At dinner they had some fun with whipped cream, even going so far as to spray it on—and lick it off—in such a way that *Blind Date* couldn't really air it uncut. Then, finding themselves all sticky and messy from the whipped cream, they decided to go back to his place and enjoy the cleansing power of the Jacuzzi. Now, in most hot tub dates, the hot tub is where things get hottest and heaviest. But it was only an appetizer for Kelly and Jerry. They moved on from the Jacuzzi into the shower—naked—and the situation, as so often happens in the shower, got simultaneously really clean and really dirty. The strange thing was that Kelly liked Jerry a whole lot more than Jerry liked Kelly. In fact, he was later set up on a second chance date with DeNiece—remember her? She's the one who flashed everybody in sight—except her date. DeNiece and Jerry made the most of their second time around. Let's just say that this time she flashed her date.

In fact DeNiece and Jerry's date ended up in the Jacuzzi, as well. Jerry came off a little like an obnoxious bad boy his first time around, but his attraction to DeNiece was immediate—and somehow she brought out the gentleman in him. These two were peas in a pod, burping in unison at dinner, trading bawdy jokes and stories and having a blast. DeNiece couldn't understand the thick cockney accent half the time but she didn't care—they were communicating just fine. In fact, they never talked of anything of substance all night long. But even so, they totally fell for each other. By the end of the night, they were making out in the hot tub with DeNiece's thong bikini barely hanging on for dear life. This time, it turned out the second time was the charm.

On one of the show's dates from Toronto, Canada, Jonathan was another man who didn't quite know how to take his date. Leena made sure that he knew she lived life on the edge, she loved adventure, and that she had no objection to a little casual sex. In fact, at every opportunity, Leena turned the conversation toward sex, and Jonathan kept changing the subject back to safer topics. They seemed to get along fine, but Jonathan seemed determined to keep things on a platonic level. Eventually, they ended up in a Toronto hot tub, where they did a little kissing, and then he walked her back to her hotel room. She seemed shocked that he didn't even try to come in. Afterward, he told the *Blind Date* cameras that they were just too different and would have problems in building a relationship.

Jessica and Chad found themselves in exactly the opposite situation. He was really, really interested in her and she didn't think a lot of him—and she wasn't afraid to let him know it. In fact, at dinner, she actually came out and told him that it just wasn't happening for her. But Chad wouldn't give up. He convinced her to go to the Jacuzzi with him—and once there, they started making out. But it wasn't really clear why Jessica engaged in that activity—once the date was over, she repeated that she had no interest in going out with him again.

Kiki and Jeff had one of the oddest dates ever, and one of the bumpiest roads to the Jacuzzi in memory. The date started out nicely enough when Kiki and Jeff learned how to make apple pie—and Jeff actually showed some talent for it. He also showed some talent for drinking too much at dinner. He got tipsy and Kiki got angry with him—so angry, in fact, that she started shouting at him and then stormed out of the bar. When she returned, they made their peace and headed back to the hotel, where they ended up in the hot tub. After all the shouting and bitterness, they somehow got around to romance. Out of nowhere, Kiki decided to kiss Jeff—just another testimonial to the magical healing powers of the hot tub.

The twins share a brain

Twin Fact

Flame and Xavier had more in common than just their peculiar names—they hit it off right from the start. Almost from first sight, it was inevitable that they would wind up in the hot tub. They started things off by sharing some coffee. They were already holding hands and getting intimate right off the bat. Then it was on to a recording studio, where they played the bongos and he got romantic, free-styling a rap just for her (see "The *Blind Date* Songbook" page 27 for the lyrics to his rap).

Things got even more romantic over dinner, as he described just how attracted he was to her and how in awe of her body he was. She liked hearing him say these things, but she made sure that he knew how much she hates players. Xavier? A player? Come on . . .

Finally, they ended the night in the Jacuzzi. Xavier asked Flame if she would consider taking off her bikini top and she replied, "Help me untie it." If any words spell "Happy Ending" more than those, I'd like to hear them. This was another genuine *Blind Date* love connection. Flame and Xavier said that they just couldn't wait to see each other again!

Jack and Jenna also had a hot time in the old hot tub. They hit it off early in the date. They went, for some reason, to wash a monster truck, and made the most of the experience by getting up close and personal, not only with the truck but with each other.

Jenna even sat on Jack's shoulders in an attempt to reach the truck's nether regions. She apparently affected Jack's nether regions, too.

And speaking of nether regions, both Jack and Jenna then got theirs checked at a medical exam—another activity we don't necessarily recommend for a first date, even though it seemed to work out just swell for these two.

The doctor told them that their bodies were in just fine shape, but Jack and Jenna had already figured that out—and after dinner, they proved it further by taking a dip in the Jacuzzi. Those bubbles make little girls do nasty things, and soon the bikini parts were flying. Jenna wound up totally naked and Jack made the most of the situation by showing her how to pose "like the girls in the magazines."

Of course, sometimes it's the guys who get totally naked in the hot tub—and that isn't always a good thing. *Blind Date* set up twins Cassie and Maile with two unsuspecting guys, Rossi and Peter. Each couple went off on their own at first and then the girls surprised their dates by showing up at the same bar. The guys immediately understood the mathematical possibilities of being on a double date with two hot twins and stepped outside to carefully plot the next step. Their plan was deceptively simple—get the twins into the Jacuzzi and who knows what kind of X-rated action would ensue.

Cassie and Maile agreed immediately to a steamy dip. Once they were in the hot tub with two very happy guys, the twins hugged and kissed each other—in an innocent, sisterly way, of course—and Rossi and Peter knew that they had just hit pay dirt.

They were so sure, in fact, that both guys removed their swimsuits and encouraged the girls to do the same.

But they didn't.

Instead, Cassie and Maile got out of the hot tub, walked across the room, picked up the guys' trunks . . . and left. This left two very naked, very annoyed guys finding out just how cold the hot tub can be.

Rachel didn't play such a cruel hoax on Jeff—they had plenty of fun in the Jacuzzi. But she had earlier sworn that she would do no such thing. One of their first stops on the date was to take a lie detector test. Rachel was asked if she saw herself "getting nekkid" by the end of the date—and she said, "No." The polygraph examiner pointed out that her answer showed clear deception. In other words . . . "Yes."

Dr. Date Says: This guy's my hero

By the time they ended up in the Jacuzzi, it was pretty clear that the polygraph examiner knew his stuff. Rachel did indeed get nekkid—and so did Jeff. And when it came time to say goodnight, they didn't. A love connection indeed.

The same can't be said for Lola and Todd. It was pretty clear to both of them early on that this was no great match. But even though Todd considered Lola to be bad-tempered and high-maintenance, he was determined to see as much of her as humanly possible. After all, bad-tempered is one thing, but Lola in a bikini is quite another.

Lola turned out to have no problem in accommodating him. Soon they were in the hot tub and she was wearing tiny scraps of fabric that could almost qualify as a bikini. Todd was a very happy guy. So happy, that he actually started to think that he had a chance with her. They jumped into the adjacent swimming pool

and Todd pulled one of the oldest ones in the book. He suggested that they pretend that she's drowning and that he's going
to save her life. In saving her, of course, he had to apply mouth-
to-mouth resuscitation. Lola screamed, "You're not supposed to
use your tongue in mouth-to-mouth." Which is probably why so
few young people want to become paramedics.

At any rate, there was plenty of teasing and playing going on in
the pool and the hot tub—but playing was really all it was. These
two never saw each other again. But Todd had no complaints—
he saw what he wanted to see in the first place.

A constant source of wonderment when watching *Blind Date*
is how many people seem to be completely free and open with
their bodies, and completely closed off otherwise. Selen and
Jaime seemed to have absolutely no interest in each other, except
for a physical attraction. This Florida couple did a photo shoot on
the beach. She took her shirt off for some of the photos and used
his hands as a kind of bra for others. And this was within an hour
of when they met.

At dinner, they could barely think of anything to say to each
other and couldn't even hide their boredom. But still, they went

on to the hot tub, where they kissed and snuggled and got naked and kissed some more. All of which led to . . . nothing. In their post-date interviews they revealed that neither really wanted to see the other again.

As you have seen, the Jacuzzi can be the source of love and togetherness, a temporary playground for a night, or a pool where some dreams come true and others are shattered. There have been Jacuzzi moments on *Blind Date* that range from the disgusting to the exhilarating, and everything in between. But if there were an award given to "Most Memorable Hot Tub Scene" on *Blind Date,* it would have to go to Kyle and Liz.

Now, Kyle was on a second-chance date, for some reason, and from the very beginning, his constant sarcasm and dirty talk kept Liz slightly off balance. At times, she seemed repulsed by him, but little by little, she started to like him.

When he suggested that they go visit the Jacuzzi, she agreed. But when she caught her first sight of him—wearing only a sock—she started to question whether this was such a good idea. Liz seemed more than a little nervous and uncomfortable as Kyle just bulldozed his way through the proceedings.

What You Didn't See

And then he asked Liz if she wanted some company. He made a cell phone call and, moments later, *five* beautiful women in bikinis arrived. By the way they acted with Kyle, it seemed that all of his sexual bragging just might have had some basis in truth. Some of this scene aired on *Blind Date* and some didn't—most notably the nudity, the girl-on-girl kissing—which Liz participated in—and the part where Liz gave Kyle a good spanking. Now that, dear reader, is a hot tub experience to remember.

♥♥♥♥♥♥♥♥♥♥♥♥♥ ♥♥♥♥♥♥♥♥♥♥♥♥♥

Actual Virgins and Born-Again Virgins

Do's and Don'ts if You're the Virgin:

DO . . . share this information with your date as soon as possible.

DON'T . . . greet every attempt at intimacy with a loud squeal, a slap on the hand, and a firm, "No way, José!"

DO . . . discuss this issue, so that your date will fully understand your point of view.

DON'T . . . rub your virginity in your date's face. Unless asked.

DO . . . explain the moral, religious, or physical reasons why you have made this choice.

DON'T . . . respond to every question with, "That's for me to know and you to find out."

DO . . . try and understand that your date might have a completely different outlook on the whole virginity issue, and may question not only your motives but your sanity.

DON'T . . . repeatedly sing "Never Gonna Get It" no matter how catchy the beat is.

Do's and Don'ts if You're Dating a Virgin:

DO . . . show that you understand what a difficult choice this is.

DON'T . . . cry, plead, or beg.

DO . . . try and find wholesome activities that will keep your mind out of your date's virginity.

DON'T . . . go anywhere that is more than a single mile from a cold shower.

DO . . . share supportive stories about when you were a virgin, and how rough sixth grade was for you.

DON'T . . . try to get your date all liquored up.

DO . . . try and determine exactly what your date's definition of "virginity" is. You know, the Webster dictionary kind, or the President Clinton kind.

DON'T . . . offer cash or other forms of trade goods in exchange for your date's virginity.

DO . . . tell your date that you understand a lot more young people are choosing virginity these days.

DON'T . . . make up stories about an epidemic of virginity-related deaths that have been kept out of the mainstream media.

DO . . . be patient and affectionate and accepting.

DON'T . . . drool.

Because, the conversation is likely to have already veered into areas of sex, it might be a good idea at this point to bring up the "V word," if appropriate. Of course, we're talking about virginity (or, if your Blind Date occurs when you're over 65, Viagra). To watch some of the couples on *Blind Date,* you'd think dates consist of nothing but sex, as in having, talking about, or hoping to have. But even among the Jacuzzi's, beaches, and games of strip soccer that characterize many of the steamier *Blind Date* episodes, you'll find some singles who, while interested in sex, still want to put it on the back burner, which, come to think of it, sounds painful. You think virginity is an outmoded concept, practiced only among some of the more conservative members of the Religious Right? Well, that shows what you know. It just so happens, virginity is back in a big way. It's so hip, in fact, that people who aren't even virgins are now virgins, somehow.

Basically people who don't have sex fall roughly into these categories: virgins, celibates, born-again virgins, and *Blind Date* producers. What's the difference, you ask? Well, the definition of a virgin changes from virgin to virgin. Technically, it means that the man or woman or boy or girl in question has never engaged in sexual intercourse—but you have to admit that leaves a lot of loopholes.

Celibates are people who have willingly forsaken sex for varying periods of time. Usually they do this unthinkable thing on grounds of religion, morals, or, as a psychologist might put it, an attempt to avoid that icky feeling that comes from too much fooling around. And, of course, there are always people who *call* themselves celibate because they want a really good excuse for why they can't get laid.

Born-again virgins are a lot like celibates, but a lot less likely to be priests. These people have already crossed the sexual frontier or, if you will, unbuckled the Bible Belt, but have decided to carefully retrace their steps—like walking backward in the snow—and pretend the whole intercourse thing never happened. Please be aware, however, that this born-again virginity thing is kind of an intellectual concept only—your body can't actually revirginize itself, unless of course, you're some sort of cyborg. This is highly unlikely, however, since cyborgs virtually never read dating books.

Now, it just so happens that all people of good will applaud any of these three choices of states of being—although condom manufacturers around the world are slapping their foreheads in frustration. But be aware that, on a blind date at least, your virginity or celibacy or lack thereof is apt to be a matter of some interest to your date. It goes beyond simply answering the question that hangs heavily over most dates—i.e., are you gonna get some—but says a lot about what kind of person you are and what kind of decisions you have made about your future. And, of course, whether you're gonna get some.

On *Blind Date,* the issue has come up several times, and we have met singles who exhibit all degrees of devotion to their virginity, born-again or otherwise. Now, this is a broad generalization (and that was a terrible pun) but most of the virgins/celibates on *Blind Date* have been female. Even in these enlightened times when humans have reached their highest peak and society is perfect in every way, old-fashioned concepts die hard. And that means that holding onto, or keeping track of, one's virginity is still more important to females than to males. But that wasn't the case on the date between Elissa and Neils. We knew right off the bat which one *wasn't* the virgin, because Elissa had already given birth to a lovely little baby girl and for a virgin to do that would be downright remarkable.

No, in this case, the virgin was our guy, Neils (by the way, his name is Swedish for "more than one Neil"). He understood that this was news that had to be delivered to Elissa at just the right time and place. So he held onto his precious secret as tightly as he held onto his celibacy. But not as long. Neils didn't say a word about it while they were having a big time riding the rides at Knott's Berry Farm—turns out he has a season pass to the theme park and describes himself as "just a big kid."

But at dinner, as they shared some personal memories, Neils figured the time was right. "You know when you said you had a boyfriend at eighteen?" Neils said. "I thought to myself, 'that's a bad idea—boyfriends.' 'Cause then they want sex and you get in trouble. You know what I mean?"

Elissa really didn't know what he meant. So he spelled it out a little more clearly. "'Cause I've never had sex."

"Oh," Elissa thought. "Now the pieces are falling into place."

"I am waiting for my wife," Neils said.

Elissa said, "That's pretty rad."

"Yeah well," Neils said, "I am proud of it and it's difficult to be that . . ."

"So you think you had friends that stayed virgins as well?" Elissa asked.

"Yeah, a bunch."

"That's cool," she said.

Feeling that this wasn't enough of a sign of his virtue, Neils went on to gild the lily, adding, "And I've never drank or smoked either." And even taking into consideration his shaky grammar, Elissa seemed to like what he had told her. They ended the evening with a hug. And before he left, Elissa gave Neils her phone number.

In the case of Ana and Todd, her virginity was just a little more of an obstacle. For one thing, Ana never told him—she just acted like a virgin throughout the date. Todd was intrigued and just a little frustrated, but he really tried not to let it ruin his evening. What made it a little more difficult is that Ana is a model and so Todd's first look at her gave him certain ideas about the direction in which he hoped the date would go. He's a surfer, always on the prowl for a *Baywatch* babe, and Ana looked like she could be one—blonde, bubbly, bouncy, perfect teeth, the whole size-zero nine yards.

They did some wholesome outdoor activities like surfing and bicycling, and Ana's revealing swimwear made visions of sugar plums dance in Todd's head. He even helped tie her bikini top, no doubt believing that he would be untying it again later.

At dinner, he ordered margaritas for both of them and soon noticed that Ana had only taken a polite sip or two. He asks her if she doesn't like her drink.

ANA: "I usually drink Shirley Temples."
TODD: "But they don't have alcohol in them."
ANA: "That's the point."
TODD: "Have you ever been drunk before?"
ANA: "No."
TODD (getting a sly idea): "You don't like to drink—what *are* you passionate about? I thought for a second that it might be sex."

Ana still wasn't ready to spring the whole virgin thing, so she said, "No, I'm not a nympho. I think if I had a vice it would be that I live on adrenaline rushes. Going after what I want in life and really doing it. Putting it all out there."

That was obviously not what Todd wanted to hear. But he remained optimistic. And even more so when, in the cab ride, she spoke to him in French. When he asked her what she had said, she replied, "I said, 'I love wild sexy nights.'"

"Bingo!" he thought. "Now it's on!"

But it wasn't on. Todd kept digging and digging for Ana's wild side, hoping to convince her to do the horizontal tango with him. But if she had a wild side, she never let him catch a glimpse of it. And she never admitted to him that she was a virgin. But since they were set up for a second date, he presumably found out sooner or later.

Things weren't so rosy between Barbara and Rob. She informed him early on that she had decided to become celibate in her late thirties because of her religious beliefs. She is a Messianic Believer (it's complicated) and Robert is Jewish. Robert was, however, an open-minded type who cheerfully engaged in religious conversations with her even when he knew, early on, that the date was going nowhere.

Driving along, Rob asked if she would marry someone of a different faith if they held similar moral and ethical convictions.

Barbara replied, "Possibly, as long as I got to raise my kids in Jesus. I want to be a wife—stay home, take care of the house and garden. Raise the kids, take care of my man. I don't want to work. I want a family."

At dinner Robert said, "Can I just tell you how sexy you look and how incredibly angry that makes me?"

Barbara said, "Thank you."

Robert continued, "You know, I think you should go all the way to full Judaism—because Jews have no sex guilt."

But she wouldn't fall for it. However, the plot twist was on the way. During a quiet moment at dinner, Barbara whispered to Robert, "I just decided last week to go to Miami and get married to a boyfriend from eighteen years ago. Just so you know."

Robert, looking like he had just been smacked in the face with a frying pan, said, "That is fantastic, actually. Wonderful." But something about the way he said it made it clear that he didn't think it was all that wonderful.

In the cab home, Barbara noticed that Robert was treating her with a certain amount of coolness. She said, a little peeved, "Why is it that when guys know they're not going to get laid . . . ?"

Robert said, "I was wondering how long it would take to get to this and finally at the end of the night . . ."

Barbara: "Well, because you're being sarcastic now. Now you're being sarcastic and I am thinking, why is that? I don't think that I have done anything to insult you."

"I am not being sarcastic," Robert said. And he wasn't; just quiet. Quietly thinking, not about her celibacy, but about why an engaged woman would go on a blind date.

There was no question about why Kevin went on his blind date with Tania. He was enormously attracted to this Indonesian-born cutie from the moment they met. This was a second-chance date for Tania. She had first gone out with a fellow named Rocco, to whom she had said, memorably, "I love to hate you." And both she and Kevin hoped that the second time around would be luckier for them both.

And it really looked like it might be lucky for Kevin right off the bat. In telling him all the reasons she prefers the United States to Indonesia, Tania said one of the main ones was that in America you can talk openly about sex. In her country, she said, most people wait until marriage before having sex.

"Well," Kevin said, "that brings up the question . . . Did you . . . ?"

"I don't want to wait till marriage," Tania said, "but I want to find the right person and do it. And I've been wanting to do it since a long time ago."

"Are you a virgin?" Kevin asked.

"Yes."

Kevin said, and it was an understatement, "Wow!"

"There is nothing bad about it," she said.

"No," Kevin said, backpedaling furiously. "It's a beautiful thing."

But he didn't think so at their first location—which was a lingerie photo shoot. When Kevin saw Tania writhing around in skimpy, lacey underthings, her virginity became less of a "beautiful thing" and more of a horrible barrier that he had to find his way over, or around.

And he kept trying. For the rest of the date, Kevin could never get off the subject of sex. He grilled her about other sex acts that she may or may not participate in. He asked if she ever makes out with her female roommate.

TANIA: "She is a great kisser. See, I don't kiss with her but I watch her."

KEVIN: "No? Have you ever thought about kissing her?"

TANIA: "See, you guys are so disgusting. This is the first date and all you can ask is do you kiss your girlfriend do you think about two women touching and blah blah. So what was your question?"

KEVIN: "Gee, I forgot in all this commotion."

TANIA: "I just want to make sure that we are absolutely clear you are not expecting that we are going to go home and sleep together or something."

Kevin lied, "Absolutely positively not."

TANIA: "Just in case, I want to tell you ahead."

They had a polite goodnight and Kevin walked away, frustrated.

Later, Tania told the *Blind Date* cameras: "Even though I'm a virgin it doesn't mean that I'm not fun. And he has no idea of what kind of fun he's missing."

Before her date with Mark, Katelin hadn't missed out on any kind of fun at all. But she had recently decided to turn over a new leaf and, if not actually reclaim her virginity exactly, at least to remain celibate until she met Mr. Right.

Mark and Katelin got pretty cuddly over the course of the date and over dinner she regaled him with racy stories about her wild past. Mark was particularly stunned by her story of a boyfriend who liked to chain her up, tie a ball in the mouth, you know, standard S & M, B & D, and T & R (all right, we're just making up initials now).

But just as Mark was thinking that he had just struck the mother lode, she dropped the other shoe: "I'm celibate now."

He looked down and said ruefully. "From one extreme to the other."

But actually, her confessions seemed to bring them closer together. After dinner, they went to a candy shop, where they painted each other in chocolate, licked each other's fingers, and gave each other sweet (literally) kisses. "That was a first for me," Katelin said.

Mark pretended to be astonished. "Really?!?"

At the door, they kissed even more passionately, then went inside to talk or something. We don't know for sure, but a good guess is that they talked a lot about her celibacy.

There were definitely mixed signals on the date with Matt and Kristen as well. Matt was really feeling the physical connection with her, but at dinner she sprang the bad news that she had been celibate for two years, calling herself a "born-again virgin."

He asked if she had ever been tempted to have a one-night stand and she replied, "Yes and no. I know that I would regret it, because I can't have sex without emotions being involved."

Matt's thought bubble: "Does 'horny' count as an emotion?"

Kristen continued, "For a one-night thing I think it's such a waste. It's such a beautiful thing between two people who love each other and that's what I want to wait for. I'm so boring!"

"No," Matt lied, "that's not boring at all. That's cool."

"But you know what?" Kristen said. "I'm clean."

Matt realized at this point that he definitely would not be getting real lucky tonight, but he still held out hope for getting kind of lucky.

"So," he said, "are you shy to fool around or do anything sexual?"

Throwing gas on the fire, Kristen said, "I have no inhibitions, once I'm comfortable with the guy. Oral, I don't count as sex."

Suddenly, Matt seemed much, much happier. And when she gave him a nice kiss in the cab, he seemed happier still. They had a warm goodnight with promises for a second date.

Heather wasn't a born-again virgin like Kristen—she was the real deal. "I've set a standard for myself," she said, "and I'm going to stick by it. Some guys get offended, and that's kind of how I weed 'em out."

Heather's date Corey seemed like the right guy for her. He said, "I love a challenge. I can't respect a girl who sleeps with me on the first date."

Corey found out about Heather's pure state mere moments into the date when he asked if she had any children.

She laughed and said, "My god, no. Homegirl (she called herself 'homegirl,' for some reason) would be the Virgin Mary if she had kids, okay?"

This took a moment to sink in, but eventually Corey got what she was driving at. "You're a virgin?"

"Yeah."

"No way! I didn't think there was any more of you guys left."

"Well, there's one for sure. I have too many things going on in my life. It just doesn't interest me right now. I am not like at my peak where I need it."

"Well, that's cool," he said, meaning just the opposite. "Wouldn't do it if I were you. 'Cause once you do it, you'll never want to stop."

She replied, "I know. My friends tell me all about it."

Corey tried to assure her. "I'm not going to try and have sex with you. Don't worry about it. It's okay."

She said sternly, "I *know* it's okay."

"Oooh, all of a sudden I feel the tension," Corey said.

"No tension," Heather said. "But I know what you mean."

Corey smiled and said, "We'll still have fun." But you could tell he didn't mean it.

And, indeed, they didn't have a lick of fun. This was one case where the virgin confession just sucked the air out of the date. And, of course, it didn't help that Corey and Heather just weren't compatible in any way, shape, or form.

But David and Shana were very compatible. When the Harvard grad told her that he had made the decision to be celibate until marriage, she was thrown for a tiny loop. "So you're a virgin," she said.

"I didn't say that. I said I don't want to have sex until I get married."

"That's good," Shana said. "That's a good way of thinking."

"I mean intercourse," he said.

"You don't have intercourse. Go ahead. Enlighten me."

"Well," David said, "there's other things you can do."

"But no sex, honestly?"

David said, "I've sowed my oats."

But, at the end of the date, neither of them was sure whether he would be sowing any more oats with Shana in the future. They were both pretty noncommittal, but, according to Shana, David's celibacy didn't have anything to do with it. And who knows? Maybe she was right.

As you can see, sometimes abstaining from sex can make a date just as interesting as grabbin' for the nasty. That is, if "interesting" is what you're going for.

Ride Home

DO . . . drive carefully—you're carrying precious cargo.

DON'T . . . make your date ride on the sun roof.

DO . . . say nothing if you can't say something nice.

DON'T . . . speak in an endless string of obscenities unless you're a famous rap star.

DO . . . see if your date is open to sharing a kiss.

DON'T . . . surprise your date with a wet willie.

DO . . . try to interpret your date's romantic body language. Or, if dating a foreigner, try to interpret your date's verbal language.

DON'T . . . say anything in any language that could later land you in court.

DO . . . be clear about your own desires and expectations.

DON'T . . . actually remove your pants in the cab. Unless specifically requested to. And not by the cab driver.

DO . . . bask in the warm feelings as a wonderful date comes to an end.

DON'T . . . tear at your hair and scream, "When? When will this hellish nightmare be over?"

The ride home is a moment of summation for the date. It brings everything together and serves as a kind of synopsis for just how the date has gone. If everything has gone well, the couple will be smiling, joking, or, perhaps, holding each other close and making plans for the future. Sometimes, couples who have *really* hit it off start making out like bandits. But if things didn't go so great, that ride can be a very long one indeed, filled with, at best, silence and, at worst, anger and bitterness. The "do's," in that case, are pretty self-explanatory and don't really require any case studies. If you like your date, hugging, hand-holding, and kissing is the way to go. Or, if that's too physical for a first date, a nice smile and a "I had a wonderful time" will suffice. What you might not want to do is to spring some big news on your date at this late hour. Rebecca and Ian, for instance, had been getting along famously. Their last stop was to watch some hot oil wrestling, always an activity designed to bring a couple closer together. And Rebecca must have felt very close to Ian because she chose the ride home as the moment to inform him that she has a young son. Ian greeted this news with shock, wondering why she hadn't told him this several hours earlier—it pretty much killed all plans for a second date.

Of course, if you didn't have a wonderful time, the ride home is really too late to do much about it, except apologize (if it was your fault) or maintain a dignified silence (if it wasn't).

Or, you might want to make your date feel even better about the fact that you'll never see each other again. Like David did on his date with Lisa. When he figured out that she didn't care much for him, he raised both legs and emitted a thunderous fart, then giggled like Beavis about it for the rest of the ride home. When they got to her door, he farted again. Classy.

Tenesia didn't do anything so rude in her last ride with Baron but she did feel the need to tell him that she would rather be with another woman than with him. Which is always good for a guy to hear. Builds up the ego.

In the backseat of the cab on the ride home, *Blind Date* couples have exchanged phone numbers, bickered, cooed, stewed in silence, and swapped spit. In one case, the couple actually swapped shirts. One couple, in a sequence that never aired on *Blind Date,* didn't like each other, yet made out in the back seat like there was no tomorrow. The guy even got to what is commonly known as "third base." Yet when it came time to say goodnight, they had almost nothing to say to each other, and neither wanted a second date.

And on another memorable date—most of which *really* couldn't be aired on the show—a man gave his date the greatest of all gifts—the Big O. And appropriately enough, after her cries and moans died out, he sang a spirited rendition of "Hooray for Hollywood."

But that kind of ride home is definitely a rare occurrence—at least on *Blind Date.* For the most part, that fateful ride is just leading up to the true moment of do-or-die, the goodnight.

Goodnight

♥ **DO** . . . tell your date what a lovely time you had.

DON'T . . . say things like "You'll pay for what happened tonight! Pay, do you hear me?"

DO . . . act graciously if the evening has not gone well.

DON'T . . . key your date's car if the evening has not gone well.

DO . . . cap things off with a sweet goodnight kiss.

DON'T . . . make out so hot and heavy that your neighbors will be tempted to throw water on you.

DO . . . exchange phone numbers if you want to keep in touch.

DON'T . . . fool your date by giving out the phone number of your crazy cousin, the one with all the cats.

DO . . . make plans for another date, if you enjoyed this one.

DON'T . . . forget to explain to your date how you'll be washing your hair, rinsing and repeating, over and over, for the next several years—that is, if you want to subtly avoid another date.

DO . . . remember to call your date later, with thanks for a wonderful time.

DON'T . . . call your date every hour on the hour for days and days and days on end. That can sometimes seem like overkill.

DO . . . rage, rage against the dying of the light.

DON'T . . . go gentle into that goodnight.

Saying goodnight at the end of your date is, in some ways, just a formality. A second date is either in the cards or it isn't. Nothing you can say or do at this point will change that. This is just the symbolic gesture, the period—or exclamation point—that tells you this event is over and characterizes to some extent just how well or badly it went.

Some of the couples on *Blind Date* didn't say goodnight, exactly. A few actually took the date inside and kept it going until morning. And a few dates just disintegrated before the issue of the goodnight even came up. You can read about some of those examples in, respectively, the "Sexiest Blind Dates" and "Blind Date Meltdowns."

But even though what happens at the doorstep is usually a foregone conclusion, sometimes it can still be a place of surprises. At least, it can be a surprise to one of the daters or the other. Fred and Kim, for instance, seemed to view their date from absolutely opposite perspectives. Fred was convinced that Kim really liked him. Kim, on the other hand, thought Fred was as dumb as a sack of bricks. At first she was simply bewildered by him. Later, she just started making fun of him. And the more she did, the more Fred came to believe that she really liked him a lot.

All through the date, Fred kept hinting that he would like a second date but Kim kept avoiding or changing the subject. He still thought he was doing fine, though, so as they were walking to her door, he asked once more if they would be going out again. Kim said, "I had a nice time, but I don't think so." Fred was totally flabbergasted. He never saw it coming; he believed that second date was a lock.

Almost the same thing happened on the dates between Andrea and Calvin and with Joseph and Shelley.

Andrea and Calvin got nicely toasted and Calvin started talking her into coming back to his place. She agreed, and Calvin was a happy man, figuring that passion was but a short cab ride away. But on the way home, he made his first move and asked if he could kiss her. She said, angrily, "No!" And that was that. Calvin ended the evening a very puzzled man. And when Joseph asked hyper-religious Shelley, "Would it be too forward if I kissed you goodnight?" she replied simply, "Yes." And she wasn't kidding.

There were no such missed signals between Rosa and Troy. They both knew that they hated each other. In fact, she wouldn't even get out of the car to say goodbye to him. He walked home alone.

Matthew thought things were going pretty well with Daniela, so he asked her to come home with him. She replied that she would love to but, "I've got to wash my hair." Just for the record, ladies, that's an excuse that works when you're avoiding *going* on a date, not getting out of a date you're already on. But then again, it worked, so what do I know?

On *Blind Date* there have been pleasant goodnights, passionate goodnights, embarrassing goodnights, and bitter goodnights. But real aficionados treasure Mark and Alex's goodnight most of all. Here's how it happened. They were getting along reasonably well from the beginning. Early on, with apparently no signal from Alex, Mark tried to kiss her. Seeing it coming, she turned her face to the side, so that he could only get to her cheek. He took this as playfulness on her part and he determined to get a real kiss later.

At coffee, Mark asked if she would like to go out again and Alex replied, "Only as friends." He told Alex that he wanted to be something more than friends and she replied, "Well then, no."

On the ride home, Alex reluctantly agreed to go out with Mark again—but only on one condition—if he didn't try to kiss her tonight. Mark saw this as an additional challenge. He told her that he would indeed try to kiss her tonight. Alex told him politely that she would appreciate it if he didn't. She even said that, if he did, she would certainly not go out with him again.

But somewhere in Mark's brain, he heard, "I would appreciate it if you didn't" translated as, "Yes, kiss me now! My lips ache for you!" At her door, he went for it. Alex politely fended him off with what can only be described as a combination neck twist/head butt maneuver. "Ah," said one of the voices in Mark's head, "she's flirting with me. She longs for my kisses now more than ever!" So he tried again. And again she bobbed, weaved, and lowered her head so that it knocked together with his in another light head butt.

"All right!" Mark thought. "She's really warming up to me now!"

He went in again.

Head butt.

Again.

Cheek.

Again.

Head butt.

Again.

Cheek.

Again.

Neck twist.

Finally, even Mark got the idea, but only after the most embarrassing and prolonged display of failed kisses in the history of the sport. And later, talking with the *Blind Date* cameras, he said he still believed that going in for the kiss was the right thing to do. Sheesh.

So, guys, remember this. One no means no. Eighty no's in a row mean you're a clueless putz.

The Best and Worst Blind Dates

♥ Dates from Hell

Now there are plenty of real romantics in the *Blind Date* audience who yearn to see the show's couples fall in love and start planning a happy future together in their suburban heaven with 2.4 kids.

But there are many, many more people—and admit it, you're one of them—who take delight in watching dates crash and burn. Maybe it's like the Circus Maximus in *Gladiator*—we still have a taste for putting people into the arena and watching them battle it out. The difference is, on *Blind Date* virtually no one has ever been eaten by a lion.

Or maybe it's just the old "better them than me" syndrome. Nearly all of us have found ourselves trapped in a dating disaster and, from the inside, it's no laughing matter. But from the safety of your own living room, what could be funnier than a real train wreck of a date? You can see it coming but you just can't look away.

Plenty of dates have gone sour on *Blind Date*. These are just a few of the most memorable. Read about them and keep repeating to yourself, "Better them than me, better them than me . . ."

Chris and Lynne

Chris lists his best features as being rich, rich, and rich.

Lynne is a 30-year-old race car driver. According to her, she's easygoing, energetic, and adventurous and is looking for a guy who is honest, funny, and has a nice body. Oddly enough, Chris, 36, is also looking for a woman with a nice body, although in his case he wants one with a sense of humor, too. Well, Lynne seems to have a reasonably good sense of humor, but that didn't do her much good on her date from hell—although maybe she can laugh about it now. At any rate, we can.

 He isn't spending his money on charm school.

Chris started things off on the right foot by giving her a dead rose upon meeting her. Or, as he put it, the rose was "half dead, like my heart." Right off the bat, he decided to entertain her with an offensive blonde joke [okay, for the record, here it is: "What do blondes say after sex?" "What were you guys' names again?"] and she sarcastically replied that she probably wouldn't understand it. And of course, *he* didn't understand *that*! Ten minutes into the date and love definitely wasn't in the air.

They started things off at the famous Rose Bowl swap meet flea market, where he started insulting her—jokingly, according to him. He bought her a hat and when the salesclerk asked if he wanted a bag, Chris pointed to Lynne and said, "I got my bag with me." Lynne informed the salesclerk—as if she hadn't already guessed—that Chris was "a sexist pig."

 Lynne is a saint for putting up with this yutz.

They then went to have some fun launching model rockets, and his rocket crashed and burned—we call that foreshadowing, folks. Possibly just to hear himself talk, Chris began to jabber B.S. about model rocket technology. After a few moments of this, Lynne explained, "Shut up!"

Chris is working on his G.E.D.

At dinner, he brought up a whole buffet of inappropriate subjects and embarrassing questions, each of which just made Lynne seem to hate him more and more.

LYNNE: "Have you ever had a girlfriend before?"
CHRIS: "They come and they go. I've found the best thing to do is just call them all 'sweetheart' and that sort of fills in the blanks."
LYNNE: "That is so heartwarming."
She was particularly annoyed when he asked her if she had ever been pregnant. "Not that it's any of your business, but no."
CHRIS: "Oh, now you're getting touchy!"
LYNNE: "Well, that's so psychotically personal."

Despite the warmth of the conversation, Chris tried to enjoy his lobster dinner ("I hope he suffered," he said of the lobster), even after Lynne pointed out, "That's the only tail you're getting tonight."

 By my calculations, this guy's a quantum idiot.

And then, the most amusing moment of the evening—to Chris and to no one else—he placed some fake dog poo on the dessert platter and yelled at the waiter about it. Lynne responded, as would any person of taste and conscience, by holding her face in her hands and murmuring, "Somebody please kill me. Please kill me . . ."

 Lynne may be patient . . .
but no one should have to take this crap.

Later, at the bar, Chris talked about his incredible social skills, calling himself a "people person," a description with which Lynne didn't see eye-to-eye. When he asked her what she wanted to talk about, she said, "How about talking about going home?" She advised him that if the occasion ever rose again when he actually dated a human woman, he might consider being nice to her and not insulting her. "Basically," she said, "this was not a great date."

At their brief and uncomfortable goodnight, she promised to think about him the next time she's driving around the race track. And we can easily imagine just how she'll think of him—as a pedestrian caught on the crosswalk.

Chris is tired of getting dumped so he sabotages dates to avoid rejection.

Shari and Kyle

Kyle flirts by being offensive.

Shari asked to meet a really sarcastic guy.

Here was Shari's first mistake. She told *Blind Date* that she was looking for a man who was "a little sarcastic." She got set up with Kyle, who's a little sarcastic like Godzilla is a little green and scaly. Kyle was crass, forward, obnoxious, and loud. He kept up a relentless barrage of wisecracks and inappropriate sex talk throughout the date and frequently barked loudly like a dog. All in all, a date from hell for Shari, but great fun for *Blind Date* viewers.

Shari, 28, is a teacher in Los Angeles. Kyle, 27, is an investment banker from San Diego. When she got to his door, he pretended to be someone else—hey, comedy, right from the start. Once he cleared up exactly who he was, he invited her inside to have sex. Oddly enough, she refused.

They got into the car, where Shari described to Kyle how much she enjoys teaching.

"Kids love me!" she said proudly.

Kyle replied, "How old were you when you lost your virginity?"

Their first activity was at the batting cages. Kyle said lasciviously, "I love a chick who knows how to handle a bat." When it was his turn, Kyle swung and let go of the bat—it went flying away. This debacle put Kyle in a romantic mood. He placed his hands on Shari's waist and said, "I'm very excited about the two of us." She wriggled out of his grasp and said, "I'm very excited about the fact that you're taking your hands off me!" It was kind of an intimate moment.

 Shari's more comfortable in the teacher's role.

In the van again, on the way to dinner, there was another touching moment when Shari informed Kyle that she is a teetotaler. "I don't need to drink because I'm naturally exuberant, vivacious, talkative," she said. "What do I need alcohol for?" Kyle replied, with his unique brand of logic, "To help me get laid. What do you think you need alcohol for?"

At dinner, the innuendos came thicker and faster than the entrees. But Shari can give as good as she gets. When Kyle murmured, "I need to get something off my chest," she fired back, "You need to get that stupid shirt off your chest. I had something like that about five years ago. It looked better on me." She informed him that she never wanted to see him again. He offered to give her a massage.

 Shari's fed up because Kyle never turns off his sarcasm.

In the van again, perhaps sensing that Shari was not completely responding to his charms, Kyle decided to give her a nice compliment. "Small breasts are great," he said. "You'll age well."

 Shari's still looking for a "real" moment with Kyle.

Despite it all, when they went for a drink after dinner, Shari kept trying to have a good time. Even when Kyle dribbled lemon juice on her arm and licked it off. The loud, disgusted noise she made pretty much summed up her feelings about the date and about Kyle.

Finally, the date was over. They walked up to Kyle's place. Shari gave him a friendly hug. Kyle took the opportunity to grab her ass. Instead of saying goodnight, Kyle barked loudly, like a dog. It's kind of a fairy tale ending, isn't it?

Brenda and Christopher

 Chris hasn't partied since his "Studio 54" days.

Well, again, it looked like a good match on paper. Christopher, 41, is a disco king with fond memories of Studio 54 and the party scene of the seventies. Brenda, 37, had fond memories of a party last night. And the night before that. And the night before that. In fact, one of the first things she told him was that she had big plans for the coming week: "I'm going to be waking up with hangovers every day." Hey, why wouldn't these two get along?

 Brenda equates alcohol with happiness.

Their first activity, possibly ill-advised as it turned out, was to visit a salon to get a scalp massage. Christopher begged off, possibly because his hair plugs just wouldn't stand the strain.

Brenda, on the other hand, pretty much ignored him and had a wonderful time being completely pampered and indulged. She explained to him, "I know I'm a good-looking woman," and "When my parents had sex that night they made the perfect child."

Driving to dinner, Brenda piqued Christopher's interest with statements like, "I'm a big tease but I'm not a slut," and "I date every day." Christopher, on the other hand, didn't pique Brenda's interest at all. She said to him, "You seem really mellow. You're like the complete opposite of me."

 Drunk guys in a bar will look at anything.

Dinner was a painful exercise in dull conversation and bad table manners, which led Brenda to make a logical comment on the evening: "This date just isn't happening." She asked Christopher if his hair was real and he countered by asking if her "tits" were real. For the record, he never answered but she did. Christopher slipped away during dinner and made a desperate phone call to a friend, saying that Brenda was "a capital L.O.S.E.R."

But it was while having drinks at Hollywood's famous Formosa Café that things started to become really contentious. He told her that her behavior was extreme and that "most extreme behavior is a symptom of insecurity." She was incredulous that he would think she was insecure.

CHRISTOPHER: "Stupidity is a turnoff."
BRENDA: "Do you think I'm stupid?"
CHRISTOPHER: No answer.
BRENDA: "I don't like guys who can't eat."

In the uncomfortable cab ride home, Christopher mentioned that Brenda would still have time to go out again that night, after their date was over. She assured him that she would. Walking to her door, Brenda said, "Sorry we weren't compatible."

Christopher replied, ever the optimist, "At least we didn't kill each other." And if that's the best thing you can say about your blind date, you have certainly been on a date from hell.

Cheryl and Ward

 Cheryl doesn't believe fairy tale romance exists.

This was a second-chance date for both Cheryl and Ward. Her first time around, she just didn't hit it off with her date. His first time around was a *Blind Date* meltdown—and Ward is the one who melted down.

Still, he seemed to be on his best behavior this time out—at first—and Cheryl started the date graciously by offering him a chocolate. But moments later, driving to their first location, he began his weird rant on how messed up the world is. No argument there, but not exactly the perfect "getting to know you" conversation. Calling himself "a hopeless romantic," Ward kept repeating to Cheryl that they are "in the same boat"—single, fortyish. His implication that time is running out and they should both settle for what they can get justifiably annoyed her big time.

 Ward takes everything personally.

And, meanwhile, just about everything annoyed Ward.

They went to a seafood restaurant and learned to shuck oysters—it annoyed him. Then they ate the oysters that they shucked. That seemed to annoy him, too. He angrily ate one, as if taking revenge on it for being so difficult to open. When not eating, he was ranting. When Cheryl disagreed with him he said, very angry for no reason, "I'm full of shit—thanks for pointing that out to me."

Would you admit you're an annoying blowhard?

At dinner, Ward told Cheryl a charming story about how his buddies just married women who could "crap out a few kids" and then no longer cared about their wives. Cheryl was horrified. But Ward repeated that he and she were "in the same boat." He said—and she didn't like it one bit—"I'm like the male counterpart of you."

Rarely is your date flattered when you point out her gut.

Ward got even smoother when they went to play pool later. He told Cheryl that he finds her attractive *because* she's old. He even pinched her stomach and said, apparently thinking this was a compliment, that she has "a little bit of a pooch going on here." Cheryl didn't kill him at this point.

Ward needs to vent less and listen more.

Back in the van, Ward turned on the charm full-blast, saying that not only is he "full of shit" but that every human being on the planet, past and present, is "full of shit," too. And yes, that included Mother Teresa. Ward chose this tender moment to ask Cheryl about herself.

She replied, "It's way too late for that."

Ward walked Cheryl to her door and was completely shocked to find that she didn't want him to come upstairs with her—he thought the date was going just fine. And maybe, in Ward World, that does qualify as a good date. But here on planet Earth, it's a date from hell.

As Ward walked back to the cab he said to himself, "Missed it by that much."

Claudia and Kennedy

This date from hell had plenty of spirit. Unfortunately, it was the spirit of '76. There hasn't been this much bad blood between a Briton and an American since the Battle of Bunker Hill.

 Claudia came to America seeking a wild guy.

Claudia, our British subject, is a 32-year-old who has kind of a Scary Spice thing going on. Her date, Kennedy, a 35-year-old airline mechanic from Philadelphia, was just plain scary.

For something that turned out to be so filled with bile and rancor, the date actually started out on a very cordial note. Kennedy showed some of his sculpture (it's hard to describe, exactly, but it brings to mind department stores mannequins struggling in a swamp) to a very appreciative Claudia. They chatted happily away about this and that in the van, and then enjoyed a rollicking frolic in an auto museum filled to the brim with antique cars. They even wore wacky hats, the sure sign of a super date!

 Kennedy's social skills are a little rusty.

Things began to turn slightly ominous during the next van ride. Kennedy admitted that he likes to chain smoke and Claudia was appalled. And since she expressed to him how opposed she was to smoking, naturally enough, their next stop was a head stop. He taught her to smoke from a huge pipe and he laughed delightedly as she choked and sniffed and gasped for air. Suffocation and potential lung cancer is a guaranteed thigh-slapper!

 A lady puffs a hookah out of politeness.

Heading into the restaurant, Kennedy was further appalled to learn that not only is Claudia a nondrinker, she's a—gasp—vegetarian. Well, this just made him mad. He finally asked, somewhat desperately, "Do you have any fun at all?" She admitted that there are some things she does like (sex: wink wink), but she made it clear that she would never undertake such a project with a drinking, smoking, flesh-gobbler like Kennedy. Now, he was even madder. So mad that he had to leave the restaurant for a smoke break.

 Claudia's lack of vices annoys Kennedy.

His cigarette didn't calm Kennedy down very much, though. When he came back in, he was more ticked off than ever.

 Having a smoke is a terrific way to defuse an argument.

"I never cared much for England, anyway," Kennedy said, "and the British in general. The British are really snooty, kind of like you." Claudia called him a chimp. With comic timing worthy of your grandmother, he called her a chimp, right back.

 Despite Kennedy's outbursts, Claudia is still a diplomat.

Riding home, the pleasantries continued. She accused him of wanting only a woman who "drinks a lot, smokes a lot, and sleeps around." A master debater, he explained his situation by telling her to "loosen the fuck up!"

Now, on the *Blind Date* episode, that was about that. But here's what you didn't see: They returned to his home, where she agreed to be transformed into one of his artworks. In order to do this, he made a plaster cast of her entire body—yep, her entire nude body. If this were any other date, you'd think that things were going very well indeed. But they weren't. After the cast was made, Claudia dressed and vacated the premises as quickly as possible. Later, they each vowed to never see each other again.

Needless to say, they remained faithful to that vow, although we must presume that Kennedy regularly sees a shiny plaster version of her butt hanging on his gallery wall. *Blind Date* later set up Claudia on a second-chance date—which went somewhat better than this one.

Jill and Eric

Sometimes, for reasons of their own, some people just set out to turn their blind date into a date from hell. That seemed to be the case with Eric. He presented himself as an independently wealthy charmer who is studying psychology. Twenty-three years old, Eric describes himself as sexy, sarcastic, and "screwed up," and is looking for a hot woman with brains and a good personality. And that's exactly what he was set up with. Jill is 24 years old and works in mortgage banking.

Jill knows the value of a dollar.

Eric's frugal with his money.

She's fun, athletic, and adventurous and is looking for a goal-oriented man with a nice body. Well, Eric had a pretty nice body, but that's about where it stopped. Otherwise, he could better be described as bored, angry, confused, belligerent, and apathetic. All night long, instead of charming or seducing Jill, he seemed to delight in tormenting and insulting her—and even, on one occasion, inflicting physical pain. Throughout it all, she seemed determined to retain her good humor, leading *Blind Date* viewers to wonder if she actually had the patience of a saint.

After a brief visit to a spa, where Eric was parboiled inside of a huge egg-shaped contraption, they decided to enjoy a game of Ping-Pong. Eric had fun hitting the ball as hard as he could, pelting her with it whenever possible. He hit one to Jill's stomach so hard that it left an angry red welt. Charming.

 A gentleman always treats waiters like dirt.

At dinner, Eric apparently ordered obnoxiousness as his entrée. A sharp and sassy waitress kept putting him in his place. Looking at his wardrobe, the waitress said to Jill, "You know, there *are* straight men in this town." He knocked back so many cocktails that he was finally cut off—always a nice way to present yourself on a blind date.

Having many more drinks after dinner, Eric reminded Jill of his pending degree in psychology and offered to give some insight into her character. However, he turned out to be completely wrong about everything he said. He was embarrassed by his failure and said, "This is the worst day of my life. I need help. I'm the one who needs therapy." With which Jill readily agreed.

 Eric doesn't see that it's too late to be taken seriously.

At his door at the end of the date Eric slurred, "Thank you for a not-so-wonderful evening." And Jill hurried back to the cab and to safety, hoping that she would one day forget this date from hell.

Scott and Naomi: "Acting Up"

Both Scott and Naomi said that they are very into comedy. But neither one of them found very much to laugh about on their date from hell. *Blind Date* viewers, on the other hand, had plenty to giggle about.

Naomi is 24 years old and an aspiring comedian who originally hails from Denver, Colorado. She describes herself as "wild girl" and insists that while she isn't "highly promiscuous necessarily," she is "a sexual person." Even so, locating the right guy can be a problem. Naomi says, "To find a guy who is a babe and can speak in entire sentences is not easy."

They care more about performing than each other.

Well, a babe is in the eye of the beholder, as the good book says, but Scott is certainly capable of speaking in complete sentences. He's 27, a stockbroker from New York, who insists that he is neither a swinger nor a player: "I haven't had many girlfriends." And the reason for this, according to Scott, is that he can't find one with the proper combination of looks and brain power: "I'm sure there are gorgeous girls out there who are smart but I haven't found them yet."

What they dislike about themselves . . . they hate about each other.

So, naturally, these two seemed to be a match made in heaven—so why did they end up on a date from hell?

Well, actually, things looked a little bleak right from the get-go. He did a card trick, promising, "If this card trick works, the date is going to be fantastic!" Actually, the trick did work but Naomi didn't seem to notice. "This is going to be a disastrous date!" She said she knew exactly how he did it and it was no big deal.

Scott asked her, "Have you ever been on a blind date?"

She said no.

Scott then asked, "Have you ever been on a *second* date?"

NAOMI: "Of course. What is that supposed to mean, funny boy? Are you inferring that someone wouldn't want to take me on a second date?"

Scott didn't point out that he was implying this, not inferring it, but that probably would have been beside the point anyway.

They then went off to a comedy improvisation class, where they made up a couple of scenes on the spot. Scott later complained that she had hogged the spotlight throughout the class. Naomi agreed and added that she didn't care.

At dinner, the anti-fun continued when they did unflattering, borderline insulting impersonations of each other, which led to this love-filled exchange:

NAOMI: "So not impressed."

SCOTT: "So not impressed, either."

NAOMI: "Why are you being so mean? I'm the most pleasurable person to be around."

SCOTT: "How are you in any way pleasurable?"

NAOMI: "Did you really just say that?"

SCOTT: "From minute one, nothing but complaints."

NAOMI: "That is not true."

SCOTT: "I can't even take this. I'm shaking in my skin, I'm so miserable."

They went to some cigars; normally a calming activity, but in this case, it didn't seem to lighten the mood any.

NAOMI: "You make me sick. You make me sick! Ewww! What are you doing? What are you wearing? Everything about you is a joke!"

 Good idea to take two cars on a blind date!

After a long, long silent ride back home, Naomi just got out of the van. No goodnight, no walk to the door, nothing. Well, on second thought, she did scream just before she went inside. Screaming is a subtle sign that you've just been on a date from hell.

♥ Love Connections

Well, after all the nastiness of those "dates from hell," it will be nice to look at some of the more positive experiences on *Blind Date*. Maybe it's hoping for too much to think that people will meet and fall in love in a single evening, but the dates that we call "love connections" come pretty close to fulfilling that hope. Not all that many of them have gone on to permanent relationships, but all of the "love connection" couples were at least smitten with each other enough to go out again and, in some cases, several times.

So light a candle and pour yourself a nice glass of chardonnay and soak in some real romantic *Blind Date* love connections.

Curtis and Adrienne

 She acts reserved to keep from scaring off men.

Curtis, 29, would like to find a woman with a big heart who's beautiful both inside and out. He's looking for a meaningful relationship and has no problem speaking his mind. He was set up with Adrienne, 27, an executive who says she's inconsiderate and self-centered—and she has a dirty side. In spite of that, she's looking for a man who can treat her like a lady.

When Curtis approached the door, Adrienne wasn't quite ready. She yelled through the door that she would be right there. And just after a toilet was heard flushing, she opened the door, seeming relieved. They hugged hello.

In the car Curtis asked what she does on a regular basis. She told him she's "sorta kinda boring" and called herself "the perfect housewife—with no husband."

They began their date like any romantic evening should begin—trying on lingerie at the Hustler store. Curtis liked what he saw when Adrienne emerged from the dressing room in a sexy leather get-up.

 Adrienne hasn't been in a serious relationship for years . . .
Curtis is ready to take that next step.

Over dinner Adrienne said Curtis gave a shy impression but she could tell that he could "bring it out." She asked when was the last time he got some and if he was currently in a drought.

He assured her he's never in a drought. He elucidated, "There's a difference between sex that means something and sex you just have."

Curtis then said, "I had no expectations for the day—yet I've been pleasantly surprised."

The two headed for drinks, where he got just a little more personal than she was perhaps expecting: "I've always said, a woman that will fart in front of me . . . I will fall in love with her."

Adrienne replied, "You have to marry me . . . 'cause I *will* fart on you."

 Adrienne's seeing if Curtis can handle her wild side.

Letting the whole "marriage" part of the last comment kind of slip by, Curtis went on to explain, "I think farting is the most intimate thing you can do with someone else. If I have been dating you for six months and I have never heard you fart then there's something wrong. I'd have to wonder what else are you keeping from me?"

Well, you can't argue with logic like that.

The romance continued and the fire burned as Adrienne explained that she never knew she farted in her sleep until a previous boyfriend told her so. She told Curtis, "I farted so loud I woke his ass up."

 Nothing says romance like the pungent smell of gas.

At this point they were completely attracted to each other—and who wouldn't be?

As if the farting talk wasn't enough to get Curtis's motor running, Adrienne changed the topic to her moles for the car ride home. She pointed out various tissue masses, noting the one near her left breast that she refers affectionately to as "a chocolate chip." She told Curtis he could suck on that one.

 Adrienne's been burned by unfaithful partners.

And speaking of sucking, when these two hit Adrienne's door they began sucking face, swapping spit, and trading tongues, seemingly reluctant for the night to end.

 Never miss a chance to pat a lady dry.

Finally, Curtis decided to pry himself away and head for home. Adrienne insisted as he left, "You need to call a sister."

Curtis replied, "I will, I promise." And, as far as we know, he did.

Jonathan and Monica: "Two Wild Ones"

Jonathan, 26, is a tennis pro, looking to score with an attractive woman who likes to play games. He was set up with Monica, 25, a teacher looking for Mr. Right but always ending up with Mr. Wrong—but not this time.

 He has a B.S. in b.s.

After they met at Monica's place she quickly locked the door. Jonathan took this as a bad sign.

In the car they talked about Vegas. Jonathan told Monica it was his favorite place on Earth. He said, "Even when I lose I have such a great time there."

They headed to the Primal Institute where they met with a couples therapist who asked them to share their first impressions of each other.

 Monica always settles for men who treat her poorly.

Monica said that Jonathan was a character, with a good personality and a great sense of humor. She further noted how he seemed to like to be the center of attention.

Jonathan, having not given quite as much thought to the subject, said that Monica was pretty.

The doctor observed that they both like attention and wanted to be the star of the show. In a rather grim diagnosis, the doctor told Jonathan, "You're manic, you like being on." Jonathan looked a little crestfallen, but she quickly assured him, "It's okay, as long as you know that."

Monica was used to being the center of attention but Jonathan's overbearing nature seemed to be working on her.

Over dinner she complimented him quite a bit, telling him that he had a good personality.

I haven't seen this much crap since the circus left town.

He replied that he's entirely aware of how self-centered he is. "If you talk, I'll listen. I'll give you two minutes, then it's back to me. All you have to do is look good. You're the woman. I don't care what your thoughts are." Luckily, he was joking. Kind of.

Monica was obviously attracted to Jonathan and she began trying to lure him with sexy stories—like the time she had "been with" two other women.

Jonathan continued to act blasé toward Monica—but that only made her more and more interested. Their attraction continued to grow on the dance floor and, later, in the hot tub. But all the while, Monica was looking for a sign from Jonathan that he was interested. She was obviously not used to being the pursuer on dates.

Monica loves a man who'll take control.

Even in the cab ride home, he wouldn't stop with the sarcasm. Monica asked if he had had fun tonight.

JONATHAN: "No."
MONICA: "Why not?"
JONATHAN (JOKING, POSSIBLY): "It's just the company I was with."

At this point Jonathan knew he had the green light. His effort to seem disinterested had paid off, leaving Monica begging for him. His mating dance began by swapping sides in the hot tub, placing him at a strategic angle to attack. Then, like a true player, he moved in for the kiss, trapping another wild creature like the ruthless hunter that he is.

In the car he was back to his strategy. He asked Monica if she had had fun.

She replied, "Yes, did you?"

He answered, "No."

"No fun at all?" she asked.

"Dinner was good 'cause I was hungry."

Hey, if it works it works. By the time they got to her door, she was crazy about him. After they embraced and kissed goodnight he said, "I'll call you, like, never. No no no, I'll call you tomorrow." And then he left.

 She's falling for another rude boy!

Aaron and Mindy

Mindy, 23, is a kindergarten teacher looking for a guy who doesn't drool. She says she's a bit naïve which leads her to be too trusting of people. Aaron, 22, is a guy you can trust. He's a nice guy from Minnesota who's working on bringing out his inner bad boy—no word on the drooling thing.

Aaron started out this date in true bad boy form by presenting Mindy with a teddy bear. Okay maybe that isn't *true* bad boy style but he did drop it as he gave it to her.

 On a first date, always let the woman beat you at games . . . and never again after that.

Their first activity was a heated session of paddle tennis where Aaron accidentally called Mindy "Mandy"—it's always a smooth move to forget your date's name. Her paddle tennis skills were no match for Aaron's, and she finally asked if someday she could be on his team.

Aaron and Mindy had terrific chemistry. Their date had a very playful air to it. After paddle tennis they hopped into the convertible *Dukes of Hazzard*–style and were off.

In the car they talked about how much fun they both like to have. Mindy told Aaron, "You don't stop playing because you grow old, you grow old because you stop playing."

 Nothing says romance like sharp instruments of death.

Next stop—a knife-throwing lesson where Mindy held Aaron at knifepoint until he told her how pretty she was. She was a natural at throwing knives but Aaron wasn't so gifted.

On the way to dinner, Mindy told Aaron he could find his porn star name by using his middle name and the name of his street. This transformed Aaron into "Michael Military" and Mindy into "Joy Martindale." He asked if she had ever considered porn as a career choice and she replied, "Well, maybe if the whole teaching thing doesn't work out . . ."

 Offering to pimp your date is the first sign of love.

Over dinner they talked about what they each look for in a mate. Mindy described Aaron's exact characteristics: brown hair, brown eyes. She wants someone sweet that she can laugh with— no wife beaters.

Over drinks Mindy and Aaron hit the mat in a knock-down, drag-out, thumb-wrestling match. She won and requested that he pay homage to her as the thumb-wrestling queen for the rest of the evening.

Then it happened . . . the moment they had both been waiting for. Finally their innocent joking was converted to outright sexual tension. Mindy and Aaron drank out of the same glass—using two straws, of course.

Mindy then lustfully peered across the table at Aaron and seductively murmured . . . "Gee, we just shared a soda pop. Does that mean we're going steady?"

 Mindy's students may have a substitute teacher tomorrow.

In the van on the way home this sugar-coated date got even sweeter when they broke out pet names for each other. She became Schnookums and he somehow turned into Poopsy. Adorable, huh?

At the end of the night, Aaron got bold enough to ask for a second date. Mindy assured him with a "definitely."

Kurt and Jennifer

Kurt, 28, is a banker who's looking to cash in on romance. He'd like to find that special someone to settle down with. He was set up with Jennifer, 29, a ski instructor trying to get over the moguls of dating. She told *Blind Date* that, although her wild days are in her past, she still likes to get crazy sometimes. And that's precisely the thing that *Blind Date* likes to hear.

These two got to know each other in the car by sharing stories about skiing and their mutual love of the outdoors. Jennifer's been skiing since she was four.

 Using glue without ventilation is a great aphrodisiac.

Their first activity was a rather unusual one, even for *Blind Date*. Kurt took Jennifer to a shoemaker, or cobbler, if you will, who taught them to build shoes. It may not have been the Eiffel Tower but it was the perfect location to start to create some romantic chemistry.

Their next stop would be the most logical follow-up to a shoe-making activity—paying a visit to a clinical sexologist (relationship therapist). Here they tried to expand their sexual horizon. They initiated physical contact by massaging each other's faces. They learned such handy, need-to-know tips as, "In lovemaking, the faster you breathe, the faster you climax."

 Kurt's trying to change his wimpy image.

Over dinner, breathing normally, thank you very much, they talked about the psychology of attraction. As they ate they became more comfortable with each other and the conversation flowed like wine. And so did the wine.

Over drinks Kurt asked Jennifer about her underwear. She explained that she was currently wearing a thong. Naturally enough, he asked to see it and, even though they were still seated at a table in a fancy restaurant, she agreed that this would be a nifty moment of sharing. So, he pulled the back of her pants and took a gander. Yup, that was a thong, all right.

Turnabout being fair play, Jennifer checked Kurt's undergarments. Turned out he was wearing boxers. That seemed right to her. She told him she didn't think he would be all that comfortable in a thong. And, for the record, she prefers boxers over briefs.

After a couple has checked out each other's underwear, what else can they do except share their first kiss? And once they've shared a nice big kiss, what else can they do but share vomiting stories?

 They're bonding over the awkwardness of the situation.

Jennifer's went like this: She told him, in rather graphic detail, how she had once puked while driving, blowing vomit all over her car. As she described how it was dripping from the rear view mirror and the tip of her nose, Kurt just seemed to fall more and more in love. If she had just jumped in with a story about running sores or nonhealing wounds, he probably would have married her on the spot.

They're revealing things they normally wouldn't. We call this the "cheap red wine effect."

At the doorstep they kissed passionately and he lifted her off her feet. They then said goodnight and began the long, slow waiting period for date two.

Well, that just proves the theory once again—the couple that makes shoes together, stays together—or something like that. Whatever it was, it worked for Kurt and Jennifer.

Being relaxed is the best aphrodisiac.

Constance and Rob: "Foreplay"

Constance is outgoing and loves to try new things.

This love connection featured Rob, who is a 32-year-old pro golfer and Constance, 33, who says that she's a former free spirit looking to settle down.

When she arrived at Rob's home, he showed her an enormous collection of teddy bears and invited her to choose one as a gift. Then he read out a poem/riddle which would lead her to another gift. She was supposed to look behind a certain teddy bear, but although the bear's name was both mentioned in the poem, and stitched in large letters across his chest, it took forever for Constance to find him. However, once she did, she found a nice bouquet of flowers just for her. Sweet.

 Rob is shy and easygoing.

In the car, she admitted that she doesn't know much about golf and he told her they were going to hit a few balls. She seemed a bit apprehensive, but actually, she had the time of her life. When she hit a good one down the range, she was overcome with glee, leaping up and down, screaming, "Whoa! Whoa! Oh my god! I can't believe I did that!" She then putted the ball—and sank it. She happily high-fived Rob and then hugged him.

 **Rob's forthright honesty appeals to Constance.**

Over dinner they talked about their family at the same moment and started to notice how uncannily similar they are. When she asked him about his girlfriend adventures, he admitted there hadn't been a girlfriend in a long time because he is "kinda picky. I look for the sweet, kind, caring, loving type of person." He told her that "exes" have done a job on his heart. "Nothing too bad. Nothing I can't overcome." He has been hurt in the past. He told her a story about the time(s) he asked someone to marry him.

 **Rob's comfort is important to Constance.**

CONSTANCE: "You asked somebody to marry you?"
ROB: "Twice."

The second time he was turned down, he was so distraught that he threw the diamond into the ocean.

CONSTANCE: "Maybe we should go scuba diving."

But instead of scuba diving, they went to a dance club. And instead of finding a lost diamond ring, they found an enormous level of terrific chemistry.

 Take notes, boys and girls, this is how it's done.

In the van, they sat very close together. Rob said, "Did you have a good time?" Constance replied. "Do you need to ask?"

ROB: "I need the ego."
CONSTANCE: "You are a fabulous, fabulous man and I had an incredible time."
ROB: "I never thought that someone like you would exist out there."

Constance, seeing that things were moving swiftly in a forward direction, said, "We haven't kissed, have we?"
Rob pretended to be in shocked disbelief. "We haven't?"
Constance added, "I would have thought we would have by now."
Rob replied, "I was going to wait till 11:20, and oh my gosh . . ." He looked at his watch. ". . . it's 11:20!"
They kissed.
Constance said with a smile, "Well, that's one thing out of the way."
At her door Rob asked if it would be possible to get her number and she said, "Of course. It was so much fun meeting you."
And they promised that their second date would be even better.

 Rob is just too nice.

Chrissy and Clayton: "Back in the Saddle Again"

This date was one of the great fluke experiences of all time. When Clayton knocked on Chrissy's door, neither was prepared for what—or who—they were about to see.

 He once had a one-night stand with a Chrissy.

When Chrissy opened the door, Clayton said, "How do you feel about surprises?" Chrissy was in extreme shock. "Wow. Whoa." She had a hard time speaking. But she finally said, "What's it been—three years?"

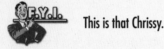 This is that Chrissy.

Clayton said, "Back in the wild days. I'm no longer wild anymore." So, what was the big shock? It turned out that they had had a one-night stand three years earlier. Clayton hadn't acted like a real gentleman on that occasion—and he never called Chrissy again.

The shadow of that one-night stand loomed large over their second date. Chrissy's bitterness came through now and then, although she did her best to conceal it.

 Chrissy still has some anger about that night.

But later, as they start remembering the details of the one-night stand—they both seemed to have especially fond memories of the shower—they started becoming closer. And when they went to a comedy club where Clayton improvised a set about his date with his former one-night stand, Chrissy actually started falling for him all over again.

At the end she said, "Clayton if you don't call me, you're a big flake." She gave him her number back at her place and they began making out—not for the first time that night, or in their lives. And before he left, he promised to call her. Of course, he promised that three years ago, too.

Sexiest Blind Dates

Okay, romantic love connections like those are nice and heartwarming and everything, but admit it—you like a little sizzle in your blind dates. There have been plenty of erotic escapades on the show—*Blind Date* does tend to attract a certain kind of uninhibited single—but it takes more than that to qualify as a truly sexy date. Sure, the following dates are filled with jiggling bodies and bubbling hot tubs, but the elements that make them sexy are a little harder to define—at least, sometimes.

Dustin and Warren

Warren has plenty of "notches" on his tennis racket.

In the case of Dustin and Warren, it wasn't so much the date it-self that was sexiest, but one of the daters. Dustin was so gor-geous that Warren seemed a little unsteady on his feet when he first met her. Dustin is a 22-year-old from Nebraska who grew up, believably enough, with the nickname, "Love Goddess." She de-scribes herself as euphoric, creative, and forward. And yes, she is a former cheerleader. Warren is a 30-year-old tennis pro who hails from New York. He describes himself as a Gemini with a dual personality. He's looking for a woman with great legs, a great smile, and sexy eyes—mission accomplished.

Dustin's studying for her Ph.D.

Warren played it cool when they went to try acupuncture—a great blind date activity!—but he lost that cool at the spa when Dustin shed her clothes and entered a rose petal bath. That image will stay with Warren—and with many *Blind Date* viewers—for a life-time. Later, for dinner, she wore a dress that didn't conceal much more than the flowers had; it fit like a second skin. Needless to say, by this point, Warren was nearly a drooling, love-crazed idiot.

Restaurant roses bought each year: 2 million . . . Number of times they resulted in sex: 2.

However, whatever Warren was feeling for Dustin, she evi-dently didn't feel it back. In the cab ride home, he made several attempts to kiss her, each of which she politely ducked. On *Blind Date,* this sad maneuver is called "the kiss diss."

Sometimes "no" means "call the police."

Unfortunately, this skin-crawling scene takes this date from the ranks of "Sexiest" to the category of "Most Embarrassing."

But it is at times like these that we must accentuate the positive and remember the rose petal bath that was the date's highest peak and try to forget about the kiss diss that made for its lowest point.

Danita and Todd

 Danita believes CPA stands for "Crazy Party Animal."

Danita is a 28-year-old who originally hails from Portland. She works as an accountant for a construction company where, she says, she has "thirty brothers." Danita describes herself as easy-going and very motivated and says that she can always make things happen. She's looking for an athletic guy who is confident, goal oriented, and has nice teeth.

 She's still best friends with her ex-boyfriend.

Hey, that's Todd! He's a 30-year-old internet consultant who says he's outgoing, energetic, and fun-loving—sounds like the male version of Danita. And his description of what he's looking for in the ideal woman sounds just like Danita, too: beautiful long hair, a fit body, and fun-loving.

These two seemed like a perfect match—and they were. They met at a bakery and headed off to a strawberry festival, where they immediately started throwing pie at each other and engaging in a whipped cream fight. By the time they left, Todd knew that Danita was not your standard CPA—unless that stands for "constant party animal."

 Nothing says romance like a fart machine.

At dinner, they got more intimate. In fact, they got very intimate. Danita confided to Todd that she likes to let her dog lick peanut butter off her—"As to where he likes to lick it off, I'll leave to your imagination." Then, she began using a fart machine to make Todd think she had gas. For the first few blasts he pretended, like any polite date would, not to notice. But he finally noticed that she was concealing something in her lap and called her on it. A good time was had by all.

 They've broken the ice by being silly . . . now they feel comfortable being serious.

By the time they went for a drink at a bar on the beach, they were acting like a real couple, with easy intimacy. Sitting on beach chairs, his jacket draped over her shoulders and his arm around her, Todd said, "I don't care what happens—we could absolutely hang." She agreed that, at the very least, they had potential to be great buddies. He said, "I haven't had so much fun in a long time."

Most guys think she's too much of a "buddy" to marry.

And then they went where they could have real fun—and a place where "just buddies" never go—the hot tub. And they didn't act like buddies there—not a bit. They made out hot and heavy in the Jacuzzi and Danita took a topless dive into the pool—if the guys on the construction site could have seen her then.

Driving home, Danita and Todd cuddled in the back seat, not saying much, but showing absolute contentment in being with each other. At her door Todd said, "I don't think I've ever been so worn out on a date in my life."

And when it was all said and done, a second date was absolutely in the cards. After all, a guy doesn't meet a girl with her own fart machine every day.

Sidney and Rutledge

 Likes men who experiment.

Sidney is a 27-year-old sex therapist who claims that, "There's never a dull moment in my world. I meet amazing people and go to amazing places. I date a lot." Although she says that she's "bitchy all the time," she also admits that "men are incredible." And, she warns, "Whoever said size doesn't matter is completely lying. Size matters."

Wants to experiment.

Which, I guess, means that she likes tall guys. Well, Sidney's date Rutledge is six feet tall—so far, so good. He is also 30 years old and a physician. Rutledge says that this gives him an edge when it comes to dealing with the female body: "I'm very well skilled, probably from my medical knowledge." Also, presumably because doctors like to work in a sterile environment, Rutledge says that he likes "clean women. I like to get them nasty, but clean to begin with."

Driving to the first activity, Rutledge told Sidney that he was in the health care field, but it was like pulling teeth for her to get him to admit that he was a doctor. For some reason he remained very vague on the subject for a long time. She told him that she runs an "interactive relationship advice" website. "Anything that has to do with relationships, we advise on it."

Rutledge asked, "Are you successful in relationships?"

"I've certainly had experience," Sidney replied.

To start things off, Sidney and Rutledge tried on straitjackets—which turned out well since Sidney later told him that she likes to be tied up. And from there it was back to his place—where he gave her a physical examination (another *Blind Date* first!).

SIDNEY: "Do you do this with all your dates?"

RUTLEDGE: "I've got stirrups."

SIDNEY: "You're out of your mind."

She looked a little concerned when Rutledge put on rubber gloves "for safe doctoring" but really enjoyed the exam. She said, "You're hired."

Rutledge is trying to balance his serious and wild sides.

RUTLEDGE: "I'm hard?"
SIDNEY: "You're hired. But you may be that, too."

At dinner, things got even more intimate (if you can get more intimate than a physical). Rutledge asked if he could touch her pants, which were made of lamb leather, then asked, "What kind of underwear goes with lamb leather?"

SIDNEY: "I don't wear underwear."

She told him that she loves being tied up and related a story about once being tied up with a telephone cord. Rutledge said, "Reach out and touch someone!"

Driving back to his place, presumably for a completely different kind of physical, Rutledge asked, "Do you like whipped cream?"

Sidney replied, "I like licking it off." Which is right up there with "You've won the lottery" among sentences that guys want to hear.

You'll be shocked to learn that things got even hotter and heavier once they were back at the doctor's place. In fact, their make-out session gained so much intensity that they had to retreat to Rutledge's bedroom, away from the prying eyes of the *Blind Date* cameras.

After the date, they gave each other glowing reports:

RUTLEDGE: "She's sexy, erotic, eclectic, and seems to be promiscuous."

SIDNEY: "He's so intelligent, he's bright, charming, got a great personality, cultured."

RUTLEDGE: "I'm a conservative guy, but a change of pace never hurts anyone."

SIDNEY: "Being a relationship and sex specialist, I would say I have no problem teaching him what he needs to know."

RUTLEDGE: "Wouldn't it be my luck to get a date with someone who's a professional in sex therapy?"

SIDNEY: "I almost threw him into shock when I brought up things that I'm into, like being tied up and blindfolded."

RUTLEDGE: "It shocked me some, yes. Finding out what she was into was not what I'm exactly accustomed to."

SIDNEY: "I think the doctor is definitely boyfriend material."

RUTLEDGE: "I don't know about long term, we'll have to wait and see."

SIDNEY: "I don't mix business and pleasure, but the doctor will be a pleasurable experience."

RUTLEDGE: "I think there'll be a lot more in-depth examination going on."

Julie and Kevin

 Julie shops Frederick's of Hollywood over Victoria's Secret.

Julie is a 25-year-old waitress who says she has a lot to offer—she's outgoing, funny, and cute. But one thing that she *isn't* interested in offering is her body. She has decided to be celibate after a very wild past. Julie says that her ideal man comes equipped with three essential items: tattoos, spiked hair, and a job.

No problem. Kevin is precisely that (well, except for the tattoos)—a 24-year-old realtor with a wild side. He calls himself wide open and fun, and his turn-ons are big boobs, blonde hair, and a good attitude. All righty then—perfect match, coming up.

 He believes every woman has her price.

They were both very impressed with each other from the start. Kevin immediately asked, "Do you have any hooker wear for tonight?"

She looked disappointed and said, "They said to dress nice!"

After an exciting session of wakeboarding, Kevin began to hint around that he was looking for something even more exciting. Julie asked, "Do you always expect sex on the first date?"

Kevin replied, "Not necessarily the first, but by the third . . ."

And then came Julie's bombshell: "I don't have sex at all."

Kevin was a little stunned. "You don't have sex at all. You're a virgin?"

"No, I haven't had it in like three months. You're like, 'can we stop the date now?'" And he was, like, can we stop the date now. But he continued.

However, Julie immediately started sending him mixed signals. When he asked jokingly if she had ever had sex with two girls, she replied, "No. I'm a dick chick."

Playing horseshoes, Kevin kept introducing sexual topics into the conversation. He asked, "Do you like to be in control?"

JULIE: "Yes."

KEVIN: "You like to be on top?"

JULIE: "Actually, I like to be on all fours."

KEVIN: "Hey, if you're not having sex, what are you doing down on all fours? We'll work with that."

Julie laughed. "Yeah, you work your charms and we'll see how far you get."

So he tried. They did a little making out at the curb, but she pushed him away.

 If he'd ease up, he might have a chance.

Nevertheless, when they were in the cab again, the conversation went right back to the main topic.

Julie said, "But when I do have sex, I like to have sex anywhere, all the time."

KEVIN: "You're like a horny little chick, right?"

JULIE: "*Fuckin'* horny! I like sex in public places, anything like that I love. Love love love love love! The most out of control places. Anywhere!"

At dinner, Kevin suggested that they just go back to his place.

JULIE: "Did you honestly think that you're going to get lucky?"

KEVIN: "Not that I thought—I am."

JULIE: "Are you that confident in yourself? Have you ever ever ever in your whole life been turned down?"

He didn't answer.

JULIE: "It seems like you wouldn't have respect for a girl who wouldn't have sex with you."

KEVIN: "That's like a main element—sex."

She suggested that they might just get to know each other in different ways, like having a beer.

KEVIN: "Like friends? I got plenty of friends."

Julie stood up and said, "I'm sorry I'm not easy."
Kevin laughed but he was exasperated. "You're making this tough—I'm having to work tonight."

Kevin can only relate to women as sexual objects.

Down at the docks, Kevin pulled out the big guns (almost literally). He did a sexy striptease for her. They kissed a lot in the shadow of a huge yacht. Kevin mentioned that the boat would be a great place to have sex. Julie replied, "Not tonight."
In the cab ride home, Kevin kept pushing—at least the guy isn't a quitter. Julie was clearly tempted by him and finally said, "Next time."
Walking to her door, he wanted to firm up the deal. "I might get lucky next time?"
"Maybe."
They had a big goodnight kiss and exchanged numbers. But you could tell by the look on her face that this date was ending just in time. Julie was strong, but she wasn't made out of stone.

Laurie and Mike

In the annals of *Blind Date*'s sexiest dates, this one will have to go down in the record books. Laurie and Michael started things off hot, moved on to one hot location after another, and ended up in a goodnight scene that was just a hop, skip, and a jump away from a porn movie. You want to talk raw animal attraction? No other couple in the history of the show ever had as much, as soon.

Laurie is 26, and works as an office manager. She describes herself as sexy, fun-loving, and classy, with an emphasis on sexy. Laurie is looking for a man with a great smile, a sense of humor—and one who smells nice.

We have no documentation on how Michael smells, but he seemed to be aces in the smile and sense of humor departments. He is 28 years old and works as a personal trainer. He describes himself as outgoing, athletic, and patient. His ideal woman is honest, affectionate, and funny.

 A normal date begins with pleasant conversation.

He didn't mention anything about breasts when he talked about his ideal woman, but if he had, he would have known within seconds if Laurie was the girl for him. She elected to walk up to his door with her shirt completely unbuttoned, so that her bosom was allowed to run free and wild in the open air. Needless to say, Mike was very, very impressed with his first sight of her.

What You Didn't See

(*Note:* If you saw this date on the show, you'll notice that she's actually wearing her shirt. That's because the spoilsport producers made her do it again so they could show the scene on *Blind Date*. Killjoys.)

 Nothing says you care more than "Can I see your nipples?"

Once in the van, Laurie explained, "I like to surprise people." Mike mentioned that he wore nipple rings and she asked to see them. She said, "Do you like having them sucked on?"

While they were on the subject of nipples, Mike decided to make a request of his own. "Can I see your nipples?"

What You Didn't See Galore

They hide behind sex rather than reveal them-selves.

Laurie said, "Ask and ye shall receive." And he did. Laurie con-tinued to ride topless in the passenger seat for quite a while.

Their first stop was at a car wash where these two made wash-ing the Expedition look like something out of *Boogie Nights.* They soaped each other up, then got suggestive with the hoses; she rode on his shoulders—in short, they got really dirty, even as the SUV was getting very clean.

They went back to his place to change clothes and ended up making out on the couch. We're talking *really* making out.

At dinner, they got even more intimate, if that's possible. Laurie said, "Let's talk about being physical. My big thing physically—and honey, you got it covered—is this area right here." She touched his chest in a provocative manner.

With Laurie and Mike, it's all physical and no mental. Maybe that's for the best.

Mike, obviously thinking that it's a small world, replied, "Well, my big, big thing—is this." He touched her chest. "So far, so good."

Then Laurie decided to share with him how she loves giving oral sex. Mike was astonished at the coincidence. "You know what's funny? You're gonna totally trip out now. That's like *my* fa-vorite."

Laurie said, "I would love to dance for you. I'd kiss you here and here . . ." Finally, her imagination got so worked up that she said desperately, "Can we go now?"

They don't even know each other's last names.

Soon, they were back at Mike's place. On the show, you saw them bid each other a lusty goodnight. But here's what you didn't see: Laurie did a long striptease/lap dance for Mike that threatened to melt the videotape in *Blind Date*'s cameras. That led to a making-out session that would make Dr. Ruth blush.

I think she likes him.

Laurie and Mike not only qualify as one of the sexiest dates in the history of the show, but one of the biggest love connections ever—they were crazy about each other.

Nicole and Blake

When it comes to *Blind Dates,* Nicole and Blake's definitely qualifies as one of the sexiest. But that mostly refers to the date as it actually occurred—not as it aired on the show. Because of those pesky broadcast standards, some of the most, um, interesting imagery on this date had to be left on the cutting room floor. But here's what really happened.

Nicole is a 24-year-old who describes herself as a nerd at heart, wacky and fun. But anyone looking at her would describe her as a model right out of a high-class men's magazine. She's looking for a guy with intelligence, open-mindedness, and a great body.

Blake gets pushed around by strong, attractive women.

That lucky guy is Blake, a 24-year-old from New Hartford, Connecticut. He describes himself as basically laid back . . . but still enjoys life. His ideal woman is confident, aggressive, and has beautiful eyes—in other words, Nicole.

Their first stop was, appropriately enough, at an elixir place where they sipped on aphrodisiac drinks, which Blake said had a little celery/urine flavor going on. Nicole asked if he had ever tasted urine and he denied it.

NICOLE: "Would you drink urine for a million dollars?"
BLAKE: "Yes."
NICOLE: "How about for five thousand?"
BLAKE: "Probably."

 The strongest aphrodisiac is the "Spanish Fly."

Unfortunately, she stopped asking at this point, so we never really learned just how low he would go. But she did mention that the aphrodisiac seemed to be working on her. "If this stuff really makes you horny," she said, "I'm gonna be back here every day."

Blake immediately called out to the waitress, "I'm gonna get one of these to go. I want a case . . ."

Their next stop was a Los Angeles radio station where they were interviewed by comics Tim Conway Jr. and Doug Steckler. What you didn't see: Nicole decided to make the interview rather more interesting by taking all of her clothes off. Needless to say, she was a big hit with the radio audience—one caller urged Blake not to "blow it"—and an even bigger hit with Blake.

 **Nicole sees femininity as passive and weak.**

Their conversation at dinner was fairly dull. Nicole said philosophically, "Just think, if all the sinners go to hell, it must be a happenin' place!" Blake agreed, apparently shunting aside the whole fire, brimstone, and eternal torment aspects of the whole thing. Nicole then said, "Life is too short. I want to see everything and do everything at least one time."

 Nicole says she's more macho than most guys.

And one of the things she wanted to do was hot-oil wrestle with Blake. They went to a wrestling club, soaked each other in oil, and then went at it. What aired on *Blind Date* was mildly racy, but viewers didn't get to see any of the nudity—both of them— and the hot makeout session that took place right there on the floor. In fact, most of what they did can't even be described in this book, a) because it's kind of a PG-rated publication and b) words can't adequately describe what went on. Suffice it to say, it was even hotter than the oil.

 Blake is comfortable with Nicole's overt sexuality.

Naturally, their goodnight kiss was a lulu. And they both expressed keen interest in seeing each other again. Hey, maybe those aphrodisiac drinks worked after all.

Heather and Thomas

Heather is a tall 24-year-old blonde who describes herself as down to earth, outgoing, and nice looking. She wants a man with a hairy chest who is good looking and has a nice body.

Thomas qualifies on all counts. He is 27 years old and a former pro baseball player who says he's tall, fit, and strong. Thomas is looking for a woman with a nice smile, a crazy personality, and someone who smells good. And that's Heather to a T.

Thomas has had trouble scoring since he left baseball.

These two were attracted to each other from the moment they met. They talked a little about "baggage" at first—and each admitted to having a little. But they soon established a nice, easy rapport with each other.

 Heather has a weakness for large athletes.

Their first stop was to make dream catchers—these are webs of fabric that hang over your bed to catch your good dreams and to keep out the nightmares. Research has never proven that this actually works, yet the public is still expected to go along with the whole scheme. Sorry. Editorializing.

 Heather wastes no time when recruiting a man.

Thomas told Heather that his last relationship had been several months ago and currently he dated, at most, once a week. Heather said, "A good looking guy like you and you only date once a week?"

From there it was on to the bowling alley where they rolled strikes and chugged brewskis. As Heather bowled, Thomas really admired her form. And he thought she could bowl well, too.

 She who talks about sex usually gets it.

In the cab on the way to dinner, she began describing the bureau by her bed. One drawer contains lotions, one contains "trinkets," and the last one lingerie. Thomas was very interested and expressed a keen interest in examining this intriguing bit of furniture in more depth.

Thomas actually dated "Miss April" and "Miss June."

At dinner, Thomas loosened up a little and began talking about his pro baseball career. He said that it was very easy to meet women when he was playing ball, but once he retired, nobody knew him anymore. "So I had to kind of incorporate game and learn how to interact all over again."

Thomas has had to reinvent himself since his injuries.

She told him how much she liked his hairy chest. "It's a turn-on. Oh, my god, it's a turn-on." And she proved it when they went for body shots at the bar. When he licked a huge dollop of whipped cream from her cleavage, the future of the date was pretty much assured.

Classy broads serve real whipped cream off their bosom.

But just to make sure everything was going the right way, Heather and Thomas then visited the Jacuzzi, making out in the cab all the way. One look at Heather in her tiny bikini made Thomas rise for the National Anthem. There was only one problem—the hot tub wasn't hot. But actually, that wasn't a real problem, come to think of it. They went inside to warm themselves by the fire. Yeah, warm themselves—that's probably why their bodies were so intertwined before the fireplace. And why, a few moments later, Heather led him upstairs to her room. On the stairs, Thomas said in an awestruck voice, "Oh, my god!" and you could tell that he really meant it.

Most Boring Blind Date

Tamika and Michael: "Fit for a Queen"

Tamika and Michael seemed like perfectly lovely people and maybe, under the right circumstances, they could even be interesting. But this date evidently wasn't the right circumstance. It was dull. They were dull. Dishwater dull. Watching paint dry dull. Remedial algebra in summer school dull. "Open mike night" dull. Bingo dull. Mathlete dull. Mormon party-time dull. Golfing with insurance salesmen dull. Pledge drive dull. In line at the post office dull. Morning farm report dull. Rice cakes dull. Get the picture? Not an exciting date.

Tamika and Michael visited the *Queen Mary*, which Michael described as a boat, like the *Titanic*, "but it's not gonna sink." Way to spoil the suspense, Michael. However, he neglected to predict that the date was indeed going to sink. Sink like a stone. Sink like a box of sledgehammers. Sink like Gary Burghoff's career. Sink like a dot.com stock. Sink like an anvil in a vat of oatmeal. Sink like the fattest man in Atlantis. This thing was going down. And did we mention dull?

Now, there's nothing intrinsically boring about the *Queen Mary*, if visiting a huge ocean liner that can't float is your idea of a good time. But although there is undoubtedly plenty of fun to be found aboard her, Tamika and Michael didn't find it. And didn't particularly try. They took a tour of the ship that had all the pounding immediacy of a Rorschach test without any of the meaning or insight. And then they ate dinner. And that was pretty much the date.

Their outing was so boring, in fact, that it had to be beefed up with provocative clips from more exciting blind dates just to keep the show's viewers from slipping into a restful and protective sleep.

Highlights: Tamika worried about getting pepper stuck in her teeth. Michael told an anecdote about the day, "seven or eight years ago," that he realized that there are onions in onion rings. He said when this epiphany was revealed to him, he was "with friends or whatever." Things almost got interesting when Tamika asked Michael if he was bisexual. He said no. She followed up by asking, "Do I have pepper in my teeth *now*?" Tamika later mentioned that she feels that she looks like a lion, especially "at perm time."

Did they ever go out again? No one could work up enough interest in them to ask.

Weirdest Blind Dates

On good blind dates, love is born, a relationship is established, and happiness reigns. On even better blind dates—dates from hell—the air is filled with anger, bitterness, despair, and horror—come on, that's funny.

But some dates just kind of defy definition. Sometimes they might qualify as love connections, sometimes they may disintegrate into horrible meltdowns . . . but mostly they're just weird.

Now, that weirdness doesn't come from their activities—although, certainly, *Blind Date* has sent its couples to some pretty weird locations. And it doesn't necessarily come from the circumstances under which the couples are meeting. No, it usually has to do with the personality of one of those daters. For whatever reason, they're just a little off.

Not that that's necessarily a bad thing. Nothing makes for better television than genuine weirdness. It might be a little uncomfortable for the, well, normal member of the couple, but it spells pure fun for the home viewer.

The following will reintroduce you to several people who left their dates scratching their heads in puzzlement, or beating their heads against a wall in frustration. We don't know what these folks are like in "real life"—but in the world of *Blind Date,* they're pure gold.

Eliza and Mike

Eliza and Mike might not necessarily call their date weird. But Mike might—in fact he did—call his date Eliza weird. However, don't get all huffy about his rudeness—he wasn't saying anything about her that she didn't say about herself. And try to prove about herself.

In fact, Eliza's exact words when describing herself were "mental case." That might be a little harsh, but she sure went out of her way to live up to the description. It wasn't altogether clear what Eliza did for a living, but it seemed to be related to rock 'n' roll in some way. Maybe that's just because she's living that rock 'n' roll lifestyle.

 Mike's totally focused on work and fitness.

Mike, on the other hand, is gainfully employed as a computer animator. He is a quiet and thoughtful kind of guy who likes to keep in shape and have interesting conversations. Yup, on this date he was totally out of luck.

 Eliza panics when she's out of her element.

First off, they went to do some volunteer work at a food kitchen for the homeless. Sure, having no home and no job is no picnic, but Eliza had her own problems—the hair net she had to wear while serving the food was really messing up her hair. Mike asked her, in the spirit of open dialogue, "Are you crazy?" and Eliza replied, "Probably clinically insane." On the list of sentences you *don't* want to hear your date utter, that one has to be way up at the top.

Next, they moved along to a Pilates class where Mike worked seriously at his exercises while Eliza mostly exercised her mouth, whining and complaining without stopping to take a breath.

 **Eliza seeks attention through sulking.**

ELIZA: "For the most part I'm pretty nice . . . in my element."
MIKE: "Where's your element? Let's go there."

She had more whine at dinner, but at least was aware enough of the situation that she kept telling Mike how sorry she was for him that he was stuck with her. Again, not a really good blind date attitude. Their dinner conversation went along in this vein pretty much throughout:

MIKE: "Do you feel the need to bring attention to yourself?"
ELIZA: "Girls are weird. I'm weird."
MIKE: "So what are your feelings so far?"
ELIZA: "I feel irritated, restless, uncontent, and slightly annoyed. I feel sorry for you. I'm moody."

Mike, beginning to feel that the date might not be all he had hoped, suggested going to a local nightspot and riding a mechanical bull. Eliza reluctantly agreed to accompany him but refused to ride the bull. Or to even pretend to have fun. However, the bull riding worked out all right for Mike—he met another young lady at the bar and struck up a brief, but promising, conversation.

Mike and Eliza rode home nearly in silence. Which, if you think about it, is actually a notch above whining and complaining.

Veronica and Derek: "Pass the Fava Beans"

Derek might look back on his date with Veronica as one of the strangest events in his life—but at least it was unique. The chances that he will ever run into anyone else like her are remote at best. It wasn't so much what Veronica did, but what she said that made her so special, and it started even before her date with Derek. During her first interview with *Blind Date,* she said, "The ideal guy is someone who looks like he hasn't eaten in a long time." Now, that may just sound like she likes her men to be thin. But later, you'll learn that this isn't quite the whole story.

Derek worked his way through college.

 Veronica loves custom-made clothes.

At any rate, Derek seemed to be slim enough to get along with Veronica. He describes himself as a "life of the party type" but doesn't spend much energy on exercising the old noggin: "I'm not made for school," he said.

Since Derek isn't much for learning, it probably didn't bother him much that he never did learn what Veronica did for a living. All he knew was that she had spiky hair with flowers planted in it, and a rather intense smile. And she explained early on how she is able to live in her nice apartment without any means of support—she sponges off mom and dad. Veronica told Derek that she periodically calls her parents and tells them that she loves them. That's code for "I want money."

She further told him that she hadn't been out on a date in two years. She recently had a boyfriend, but broke up with him a few months ago. And, although it didn't seem to have anything to do with her recent breakup, Veronica explained that her religion is "Pagan Buddhism," whatever that is, and that she's a vegetarian. But she eats fish. When they got to dinner, she claimed to be very hungry but she stressed that she won't eat chicken. In fact, she said, "I don't like to eat anything with a face." Apparently when she said she ate fish, she was speaking of that rare faceless breed that's becoming so popular now.

And while Veronica was on the subject of food, she added, "I have this weird phobia where I don't like eating in front of people. I like to eat at home, alone in a corner when no one's watching."

 Derek's projecting his feelings about the date.

Therapy may not help!

DEREK (capturing her essence in a single concise sentence): "That's kind of creepy."

VERONICA: "I feel like everyone around me is energy and their energy's in my food and when I eat, I'm eating them. Or the essence . . ."

DEREK (clearly disturbed, but smiling calmly and making no sudden moves): "Wow, that's a problem. You might want to go to a therapist for that."

VERONICA (on a roll now): "I like to drink people. So I feel like everyone is in my red wine. Yeah. Everyone tastes pretty good."

By this point Derek might have believed that he was as creeped out as possible. But he was wrong. In a moment she looked deeply into his eyes and said, "I never want to leave. I just want to sit here with you for an eternity."

Thinking quickly, which even he admits is not something he does a lot of, Derek replied, "Oh, how sweet. I think it's time to hit a club."

VERONICA: "There's no intimacy."

DEREK: "There's tons of intimacy. Let's go to a club."

So they went to a club and actually found a quiet place just made for intimacy. Trying to get to the bottom of things, Derek asked Veronica what she likes to do when she goes out, and she replied, "I like boys who like girls who like boys who look like girls who look like boys who do girls like they're boys who do boys like they're girls, and they always should be someone that you really like."

When Derek suggested that it was time to head home, Veronica mournfully chewed on two more olives (olives don't have faces) and said nothing.

She didn't say anything on the ride home, either. Neither did Derek. At her door, they embraced and he promised to call her again. Needless to say, he didn't. It's just as well, since he didn't really seem like a boy who likes girls who like boys who look like girls who look like boys who do girls like they're boys who do boys like they're girls. But then, who does?

Mark and Kimi

If you were dating an internationally famous beauty and were yourself a writer/producer/director/rock 'n' roll star/sex symbol/millionaire/author, would you come on a TV show to get set up on a blind date?

 Mark exaggerates about his success.

Well, you would if you were Mark. Yep, the above is exactly how he describes himself. Mark is 32 and says he's currently in a relationship with blonde bombshell, marrier of the elderly and wealthy, Anna Nicole Smith. He calls himself a "good bad boy" and compares himself to a role model who is just as connected to reality as Mark is: "I'm like Batman, if you would. Batman's bad but he's good. Defending faith and honor and doing things that are funny." Yep, that's Batman in a nutshell. Which is exactly where Mark . . . oh, never mind.

 Anna Nicole Smith begged him to marry her.

Now Mark's lucky date, Kimi, is 31 and confesses to having a thing for Scottish accents—strike one for Mark—and says that she treats boredom as a personal enemy. She also describes herself as "very moody and passionate" and "very intense." She doesn't like playboys, but she does admit, "I tend to live in a fantasy world." Well, that's *one* in Mark's favor, anyway.

Sometimes on *Blind Date*—and, apparently, in real-life dates—men don't open up and tell their dates about themselves. That wasn't Mark's problem. He told Kimi plenty. The trouble was, he didn't tell her anything that she actually believed. Kimi began having fun with Mark pretty early on. She wasn't impressed with his constant name dropping; she kept asking him if he was on drugs; and demanded written proof of all things he took credit for—like that hit record that no one had ever heard. She busted him on the glitter he wore and ragged on his clothes—like, if he's so rich, why can't he afford the rest of his shirt? Oh, and did we mention that he was wearing blue nail polish? Kimi mentioned it. A lot. Accompanied by sneering laughter.

Mark believed that if he continued to impress Kimi with all his remarkable accomplishments, she would fall for him like all the models, strippers, and *Playboy* playmates he claimed to date (with Anna Nicole's blessing).

Mark uses fantasy to avoid facing reality.

MARK: "Will you be nicer now that you know I'm a rich rock star?"
KIMI: "No."
MARK: "I have everything."
KIMI: "Then what are you doing here?"
MARK: "That's what I'm thinking."

And later at dinner, while Kimi shredded her napkin like someone under an enormous amount of stress, Mark asked, "Why do you hate me?"

Kimi replied, "I didn't say I hated you. I think you're weird."

MARK: "I may be nobody but nobody's perfect."

But throughout the evening, Mark would never budge on his stories of being rich and famous and Kimi never stopped calling him on it. He finally had a meltdown of sorts on the cab ride home, calling her all kinds of rude names. But since Kimi had never taken Mark seriously for a single instant of the date, his insults didn't really hit the bull's eye.

 Kimi's had enough of men who lie to her.

Afterward, they faced the *Blind Date* cameras and recapped their weird date.

KIMI: "It was horrible. It was bad. It was so bad."
MARK: "I was going through hell tonight."
KIMI: "My date was a nightmare."
MARK: "This girl's got some issues."
KIMI: "He was insane."
MARK: "Usually girls love me."
KIMI: "For someone who claims to have all the money, I don't understand why he was wearing his sister's clothes."
MARK: "She was insulting me and I don't know why. Was it me or was it something I said?"
KIMI: "Anyone who needs, feels the need to name drop that much has got problems."
MARK: "I've got an incredible girl, Anna Nicole Smith, the playmate of the year."
KIMI: "He claims he's dating Anna Nicole Smith, but just because you press pause on one of her movies, does not mean you have a relationship with her."
MARK: "I usually date supermodels or super nice girls. I'm a Hollywood bad boy. She's missing out on limousine rides, fun times, fat cash, with the exciting, fresh, interesting people that she can only read about and dream about."

KIMI: "He claimed that he wasn't attracted to me, but the whole night, he was staring at me like a mental patient."

MARK: "Stop. Come on, girl. She was killing me, man. I can't have the candy, she makes my head hurt." (Yes, that's really what Mark said.)

KIMI: "Let's see, do I want to go out with him again? Let me think. *NO!*"

MARK: "I don't want to go out with Kimi again. I don't even want to go out with Kim again. That girl is crazy."

Well, so their blind date didn't work out all that well. Kimi will certainly rebound—she says she has no trouble on the dating scene. And as for Mark—what's the big deal? He's a famous actor, musician, model, millionaire sex symbol with a hit record and a celebrity girlfriend, isn't he? For most guys, that would be plenty. But Mark is, to put it mildly, not like most guys.

Elizabeth and Elly: "Mission to Mars"

Because the show is based in California, the great majority of the singles who appear on *Blind Date* live in the state, even though many have only recently moved there from other parts of the United States—and even from foreign countries. On occasion, the show has traveled to Atlanta, Toronto, Miami, and Chicago to check out the singles scene in those cities.

But Elizabeth's date Elly just might have traveled farther to be on the show than anyone else. Judging from all available evidence, he's from Mars.

Of course, he resembles an earthling in many ways. An eleven-year-old earthling, sure, but an earthling nonetheless. Elly giggles a lot. He keeps a healing crystal near the swimming pool to purify the water. He loses his train of thought easily. And he talks like no one has ever talked on *Blind Date*.

Elizabeth knew right away that something was up. As they bounced around like kids in a big inflatable dinosaur (you had to be there), she said "You are such a freak, aren't you?"

Elly replied, "Were you looking for a twin?"

ELIZABETH: "No, but I was hoping for a twin from the same solar system."

But if that's what Elizabeth was after, she was out of luck. For in the van, heading for their next location (don't worry, Elizabeth was driving), Elly shared something with her.

"There was a vision once that I had," he said. "It was revealed to my brain and to my mind that I was so ancient in time that I was actually lava twisting underneath layers of rock, trying to get up to the surface to express its new creation in land. Then I was a brontosaurus. I was a brontosaurus munching on huge big leaves, like *munch munch munch*—just being my brontosaurus energy. It was just time to be a brontosaurus. And I was accepting life as it was."

Elizabeth just nodded at this story, pretending to understand it, but actually checking all the exits for a quick getaway.

Their next activity was, of all things, a knitting class. Elly seemed to be having a good time, perhaps psychically communing with the yarn, but Elizabeth was a bit on edge. She even said as much: "I'm tense, I'm tense, I'm very tense." Ever helpful, Elly tried to massage her shoulders but Elizabeth whispered, "Please don't touch me." Not a sign that your date is warming up to you.

At dinner, Elly told Elizabeth about one of his goals: "I would create a theater movie multi-media hall space that would have maybe a 180-degree audience but a small audience so that it still has an intimate feel. And maybe 270 degrees." Hmm, isn't that the surface temperature on *Mars*?!? But we digress.

Elizabeth's bluntness shows she's "checked out."

Whenever Elizabeth questioned Elly's stories or tried to interject a note of reason into his theories, he became defensive, asking if she's always this interrogative. "It seems like you're just bashing my like core talents," he said. "What I hope and aspire for. I mean, the fact that you think like there's no audience for what I create, too. That the general public would think I'm crazy and a serial killer and what I come up with is worthless."

"Well, it's possible," Elizabeth said.

But a second date turned out to be impossible. Elly actually asked Elizabeth for her phone number but she gently refused. He will apparently have to go back to his home planet to find true love.

Monique and Sean

In most of the weird blind dates described here, the weirdness began right off the bat. But in Monique's case, it took a little while to reveal itself. This 21-year-old beauty from Carson, California, described herself as fun and funny and a person who loves to do crazy things. And when Sean first laid eyes on her, that's pretty much what he saw, and he was pleased. Sean, 22, is a whopping six foot five and makes his living as a professional skater. When describing his ideal woman, he was pretty specific with the physical attributes—pigtails, long legs, and tight abs—but he didn't really say much about her mental or emotional condition. Maybe he'll want to be more specific in the future.

 Sean keeps a string of ladies on hold.

Sean calls himself a grizzly bear on the outside, but a teddy bear on the inside. Apparently, that's a combo that attracts a lot of women. His cell phone rang constantly throughout the date. If Sean was a bear, then Monique was like a cat. At least she sounded like one when she started making a weird choking/coughing noise in the car. It sounded as if she were trying to hock up a hairball. Luckily, she didn't.

Monique and Sean started things off at a printing press where

Monique learned about printing while Sean chatted on the phone. This may have rubbed Monique the wrong way, because when they moved on to a karate lesson, she tried to beat the crap out of him, and they fought until she collapsed. Mmm, romantic.

Sean had commented off and on through the date that Monique was acting a little "bitchy," but it was at dinner that things started coming out into the open.

Sean said, "Somebody messed you up bad. They did some serious damage."

Monique replied, "I told you, it was the moon. The full moon. That's why I've been acting like a bitch all day long."

 Monique can change personalities on a dime.

Hmm, earlier she was acting like a cat, but now she was getting into a little werewolf thang.

"Has anybody ever called you weird or crazy?" Monique asked.

Sean: "Not really."

Monique (sadly): "They've done that to me. I've been called weird and crazy all my life."

 Sean's judging Monique is a major turn-off.

Sean kept trying to psychoanalyze Monique as they were taking a cab to the next location, and she finally got a little fed up with it. "Why the hell are you trying to analyze my life?" she demanded. "Keep that stuff in check." Then she shouted, making whip motions with her hand, *"CHECK! CHECK!"*

Sean said, speaking for all of us, "You're scaring me."

He may have thought that things would get more interesting

and intimate when they took a dip in the Jacuzzi, but it was about the coolest hot tub experience in the history of *Blind Date*. They pretty much sat there trying to make more lame conversation. Finally, Monique said, "I think it's time for me to say *adieu*."

Sean was confused by this. "I do?"

"*Adieu*," Monique said. "Good-bye." And she meant it.

 Werewolves and PMS are a deadly combo.

Krista and Mike: "Too Weird For Words"

The best weird blind dates are those in which the personality of one or both of the daters is askew. The dates are somewhat less amusing if a single is *trying* to be weird. To a great extent, that was the case on this date. Mike, 26, might be genuinely odd, but he was also doing a lot of performing for his own amusement. However, you have to hand it to him—Mike can do a heck of a Scooby-Doo impression. He said of himself, "I'm a troublemaker but I know how to, I know how far to push it. Actually, that's not true, sometimes I push it too far and I either get reprimanded or fired."

Mike was set up with Krista, 23, who described herself this way: "I'm personable. I'm outgoing. I always will have a good time no matter where I'm at unless I'm with somebody who just is impossible to get along with, but that's very rare."

So, Krista can have fun no matter what, and Mike can sometimes push things too far. The stage is set.

Mike started things off on a cute note by bringing her a vase of balloon flowers. He took one look at Krista and said, "Sweet. You're cute."

One of their first topics of conversation was how much he has always liked insects, bugs, and lizards. Krista replied that she has always been terrified of creepy crawly things. There's more of that foreshadowing that we talk about so much around here. Mike replied, "Even ugly things can be beautiful."

Don't channel voices through a plastic toy.

They stopped off at a bar for a little drink, and Mike introduced Krista to his little pal, a plastic bug named Mantis. Mantis talked a little like a rich boor. After talking through Mantis for a moment, Mike dipped the bug into Krista's drink. She was amused by neither the talking bug, nor the lump of green plastic in her cocktail. She said, "I didn't like Mantis."

Mike replied, "Mantis goes everywhere with me."

Mike described his life as "one gigantic weekend" and, to prove it, they went to play around a toy store. While Mike was doing handstands and scaring little kids, Krista walked away, muttering to herself, "He's a dork."

Krista brings out her inner child now and then . . . Mike never puts his away.

At dinner, Krista was dressed nicely in an elegant dress. Mike was dressed in a conservative suit—and a weird Sherpa hat, as if he had plans to scale Everest after dinner. When Krista asked him about it, he got a little defensive. "I never said anything about that 'do me' outfit that you wore at the beginning of the date," he said.

Now, Krista was a little angry.

MIKE: "Can we start over?"
KRISTA: "No."

To make things better, Mike told Krista that he had a gift for her.

KRISTA: "I'm not into you."

Don't make your date fear for her life.

She began to open the box and as soon as she saw what was inside, closed it quickly, and leapt up from the table. Mike's present was a live scorpion. Krista shrieked, "Is that funny?" And from the tone of her voice, it was pretty clear that she didn't think so.

Mike pretended not to understand how she could possibly react this way. He said, "We fear things that we don't understand." He put the scorpion on his head.

Krista was still not amused. "Oh my god, my stomach hurts."

Mantis tried to lure her back to the table. But she refused to budge.

"I'm pissed," Krista said. "How would you even think this was funny? Seriously? Putting a scorpion that big in a box. How is that funny?" She started to cry.

Riding home—apparently the scorpion took a separate cab—Krista asked, "Are you really like this in real life?"

MIKE: "Yes."
KRISTA: "You're a complete ass."

There was no goodnight to speak of. In fact, Krista soon stormed back downstairs with his balloon flowers and thrust them into his hands.

Now, more than ever, Mike mugged mercilessly for the camera, acting and emoting and proving that he had gone through the date for his own personal amusement, without any thought for Krista's feelings at all. Maybe that isn't weird, but it also isn't nice or classy.

 Mike amuses himself at the expense of others.

Their comments about each other bore no real surprises:

KRISTA: "My first impression was that he was a dork."
MIKE: "I think Krista thinks I'm a jerk."

KRISTA: "Mike was absolutely a fool to think that a scorpion was funny."

MIKE: "Save the drama for your mama. I mean, it was a scorpion. It wasn't a rattlesnake."

KRISTA: "Mike is ridiculous, retarded, and inept."

MIKE: "I think that it was a good date. I know she doesn't think that but I think it was fun. I'll look back at this date and think it was a fun time."

KRISTA: "Mike has been the worst date I have ever been on."

 Mike, call me ASAP—you need help.

 Hold off on the wedding invitation.

Blind Date Meltdowns

It's time for a little distinction in terms here. A "date from hell" is where one or both of the parties are just miserable, where almost nothing good happens, and where both of them just can't wait for the whole thing to be over with.

A *"Blind Date* Meltdown" is when they *literally* can't wait for the date to be over—and the whole thing just implodes at some point along the way. Depending on your point of view, meltdowns are either the most uncomfortable dates to watch—or the most fun. Or, in that uniquely *Blind Date* way, a combination of the two.

Ann and Jeff

Opposites attract, the cliché goes. But this date proves that clichés aren't always right. Ann and Jeff were opposites, all right. But the only thing they attracted was one of *Blind Date*'s nastiest meltdowns.

Ann is a 26-year-old intellectual with a master's degree in foreign policy. As you might suspect, given her pedigree, she works as a pastry chef—hey, smart *and* sweet! She seems to be the only woman in the history of *Blind Date* to describe herself as "sprightly" but, in this case, the shoe fits. Ann said that she was searching for an intelligent guy who is also funny and has a steady job.

Well, one out of three ain't bad. Jeff, 25, has a steady job as a graphic designer. Otherwise, he doesn't quite fit Ann's criteria. In fact, he doesn't even know what criteria means. Jeff is the prototypical California surfer dude who describes himself as "Extreme!" and giggles like Beavis as a response to virtually everything he hears. He likes women who are tall, athletic, and blonde which, to be fair, Ann isn't.

From the beginning, these two were missing a connection. In their first conversation in the car, Ann tried to get the conversational ball rolling with a lively discussion of the European trade treaty. Jeff's response to this topic can be summed up, roughly, as "Duh?"

 Dude! Way to get her into lingerie.

They veered more into Jeff's world by modeling lingerie and playing an extreme game of paint ball. Ann tried to be a good sport throughout, but neither activity was her cup of tea. In fact, she probably would have preferred a cup of tea.

As long as Jeff was in extreme action, he seemed to be having a fine time. But whenever Ann tried to make conversation, things went south. Her jabs at his intelligence were subtle at first, less so as the evening wore on. At one point he voiced his fervent hope that she would "chill the fuck out."

 Ann was kicked off the debate team . . . for being too argumentative.

Jeff has a tendency to be blunt.

At dinner, things got even worse. Ann told him that she just wanted to make the best of things, but Jeff felt that she had been attacking him all day. She asked, reasonably enough, "Then why are you doing this?" Jeff paused, gathering his thoughts, then replied, "I'm not actually. I'm done. Later." Then he got up and stormed away. Ann seemed shocked yet amused by the outburst.

Jeff hung around long enough to tell *Blind Date* cameras that Ann was "stupid" and "pale."

Ann described Jeff as having "the I.Q. of soup."

Ann majored in diplomacy in college.

Christine and Steven

Some blind date meltdowns are angry. Some are violent. And some, like this one, are just peculiar. Christine kissed Steven. She flirted with Steven. She posed nude for Steven. She talked about sex with Steven. Then she decided she hated Steven and stormed away, leaving him alone at dinner. But before leaving, she kissed him again. As Shakespeare, the Bard of Avon, might have put it, that's freakin' weird.

Christine is a 29-year-old sales rep who describes herself as loving, affectionate, and romantic. She's looking for a guy who is extremely intelligent, a good listener, and spiritual. Well, as we've said before, one out of three ain't bad. Steven is a 36-year-old publisher from New York. He described himself to *Blind Date* as ambitious and smart. In the first moments of their date, he described himself to Christine as "a bipolar manic-depressive alcoholic." As it turns out, both of his self-assessments seemed to be accurate.

They made nice chitchat in the first car ride and Steven punctuated the conversation with frequent calls for cocktails. Even though they met in the morning, he couldn't wait to start drinking. Which he soon did.

They went to the park, where Christine agreed to pose for Steven's photographs. And pose she did, in progressively fewer and fewer clothes. Some of the photo session aired on the *Blind Date* episode but some of it could only have been aired on late-night cable, if you get the drift.

Having shared this intimate moment, they discussed their relationship a little.

 Christine craves constant approval.

CHRISTINE: "You're not attracted to me, right?"
STEVEN: "Do I think I'll spend my life with you? No. Do I think we'll have hot, great sex? Yes!"

CHRISTINE: "You are more into cocktails than me! Don't touch me!"

STEVEN: "No sex, huh? Is a hand job out of the question?"

Then they kissed. Told you it was peculiar.

Therapist Joe Says: He's a bipolar, manic-depressive alcoholic.

At dinner, Steven—pretty nice and enthusiastic up to this point—suddenly got sullen and angry. He complained about the service, even getting up from the table to find a waiter to take his cocktail order. Christine prides herself on having that certain air of sophistication, so, with a full menu of fine cuisine to choose from, she ordered a ham and cheese sandwich with French fries.

Steven's conversation veered between flirtatiousness, crudity, sappy seriousness and anger and all the way back again. He confided to his date that he's "hung like a fucking mule" and "I think I'm gorgeous, too." They kissed some more, he begged her to go to the Jacuzzi with him, he complained some more about the service and then, out of nowhere, Christine decided to terminate the date and go home.

"You're pretty dumb, really," Steven said. "You must be to be leaving me." Christine got her food "to go." But before she stormed out, she and Steven kissed some more. Then she went home and ate her cold dinner in front of the television set while Steven stayed at the restaurant, finishing his meal alone.

In their post-date wrap-up they tried to put their date into some kind of perspective:

CHRISTINE: "Pig. He was a pig."

STEVEN: "A little skinny."

CHRISTINE: "My date was horrible."

STEVEN: "She was a great woman, she just wasn't the woman I wanted to be with."

CHRISTINE: "Very repulsed by him."

STEVEN: "She had too many cocktails."

CHRISTINE: "I remained poised at every moment of the date."

STEVEN: "I think she liked me a lot."

CHRISTINE: "I didn't like this man at all."

STEVEN: "I think that she would really be totally impressed if I knocked on her door tomorrow with a flower."

CHRISTINE: "He was horrible, he was unclassy, he was just terrible."

STEVEN: "Really nice chick, good heart, good soul, nothing wrong with her."

CHRISTINE: "I felt that he was arrogant, conceited. I do not want to see him again."

STEVEN: "It's not about my master's degree, I just know the . . . I don't know [BLEEP] right now, because I'm drinking a beer without a label."

CHRISTINE: "I couldn't take it anymore."

STEVEN: "What basically bugged me about her, was, like, she was trashy."

CHRISTINE: "He's just rude. He was a rude person."

STEVEN: "No, she's not trash. She's not stupid."

CHRISTINE: "I never want to go out with this guy again, I never want to see him again, he's atrocious to me."

Which, when it comes right down to it, doesn't explain a thing about this ultra-weird blind date meltdown.

Lisa and Ward

Lisa and Ward had a blind date meltdown—but in the official record books, it will have to be marked with an asterisk. The date pretty much went up in flames, then ended on kind of a friendly note; it was a meltdown with a twist.

The first participant in this meltdown was Lisa, a 32-year-old marketing director who originally hails from Michigan. No reason to think that she would be a part of the nastiness to come, what with her describing herself as fun, energetic, and self-motivated. Lisa told *Blind Date* that she is looking for a man who knows how to dress and is dependable. And for reasons that defy logic, she was set up with Ward.

Now, regarding Ward's dependability, we have no testimony, pro or con. As far as we can tell, he's dependable as all get-out. But when you add the "knows how to dress," well, the issue becomes slightly stickier. Technically, Ward *can* dress himself. After all, he is 38 years old and a private lender, to boot. But the cardigan sweater and too-tight pants that he sported on this date probably aren't quite what Lisa was getting at. Ward said that he wanted a woman with a sexy voice, pretty hands and feet, and intelligence. Well, again, "sexy voice" is in the ear of the beholder, but generally Lisa seemed to be just what the private lender ordered.

So there was always a chance that something would come of this date. And something did. Something terrible.

Now, communication is essential on a date of any kind. And these two certainly communicated. But their give and take mostly consisted of anger, sarcasm, bile, and bitterness. Even early on in the date, the crucial time to make nice, Ward was as abrasive as steel wool. Lisa was no shrinking violet—she could give as good as she got.

During one innocent conversation about his dating life, Ward got very angry and snarled, "Let me tell you, I have never, ever met a woman that I cannot live without. And that's what it's going to take for me . . . I've never chased after a woman, I've never felt like, 'Oh! I've gotta have her!' "

Therapist Joe Says: Ward's ugly dating past has soured him on women.

Lisa responded, reasonably enough under the circumstances, "Maybe you're gay."

This did not cheer Ward up. Later, apparently trying to put a more cheerful spin on the date, Ward told Lisa that she has nice kneecaps.

At dinner, Ward told Lisa that it had been a while since he had been "intimate" with a woman. She suggested that he must spend a great deal of time—how shall we put it?—taking care of himself. This made him quite angry. He claimed when it came to, um, self care, he never had and never will. Lisa snorted with disbelief, as did most of the *Blind Date* viewing audience. He said, very mad now, "I am not joking! I don't joke about stuff like that." Lisa also introduced such provocative subjects into the conversation as, "Stop yelling—there's children in this restaurant" and "Jack-ass—shut up, you idiot." By this point, they were getting along famously. He mentioned that he's been thinking about what they should do on their second date.

At a bar, they enjoyed after dinner drinks while playing pool and bickering. At one point, Lisa forgot his name and called him Tom.

But it was Ward's tie that caused the meltdown. Dressed a little like Willie Loman in a very low-rent production of *Death of a Salesman,* Ward sported a tie that apparently offended the finer sensibilities of several of those present. One gentleman (whom later Ward described lovingly as "white trash") actually suggested that Ward adjust the tie. Lisa, getting to the point, told him just to take it off. This infuriated Ward, who responded, "Yeah, why don't I just hang myself with the damn thing." Lisa, possibly thinking that this was a grand idea, instead responded, "Shut up. You're an idiot," and walked out of the bar. Meltdown.

But here's the peculiar part. They took a cab back to his place and she asked to go in and use his restroom. All smiles, he agreed. And when she came out, there were friendly goodnights all around.

In the post-date interview, Ward said surprisingly nice things about Lisa. Even less surprising were all the rotten things Lisa said about Ward.

Sometimes, *Blind Date* gives singles a second chance if things get particularly rotten on their date. Lisa sure deserved another shot—but, instead, Ward was brought back for another appearance on the show. You can read about that one in the "Dates from Hell" section.

Martinique and Lionel

Okay, now this one seemed like a match made in heaven. But in no time flat, Lionel and Martinique's date went so far south, old people started retiring in it.

 Martinique's a totally devoted mom.

But who could have seen it coming? Consider the two singles: Martinique is a 23-year-old teachers' assistant from Los Angeles. When asked to describe herself, she uses words and phrases like "easygoing," "vivacious" and "all around fun." She's looking for a special guy who is handsome, talkative, and outgoing. Well, at first glance, Lionel seemed to be just the man she seeks. He's a 29-year-old herbalist who says, "To know me is to love me." His turn-ons include a sexy walk, sexy talk, and a nicely dressed woman. Hey, that's Martinique in the proverbial nutshell.

 Martinique's guarded about her private life.

Lionel is no shrinking violet when it comes to conversation and, within moments of meeting Martinique, introduced the subject of her underwear. When she finally admitted that she wears "bloomers" (sometimes known as "Grandma drawers"), Lionel was appalled. Still, he obviously decided not to let her enormous panties spoil the moment and continued to make sexy talk, to which Martinique didn't respond one way or the other.

Now, if David Lynch, the great director of *Eraserhead* and *Blue Velvet,* ever directed an episode of *Blind Date,* chances are the results would be something like the first activity that Lionel and Martinique enjoyed. Picture this: a young black couple playing ice hockey indoors with a dwarf, or little person, shopping for skates in the background. Yes, it really happened just that way. And surprisingly, an angry game of indoor ice hockey did nothing to fuel their romance.

At dinner, Lionel's conversation consisted entirely of what your mother would probably call "gutter talk." Even though Martinique was clearly not responding to his barrage of sexual innuendo, he just kept blasting with it.

Dr. Date Says: Date going poorly? Try hustling her for cash.

After dinner, they retired to a neighborhood bar, where Lionel challenged Martinique to a pool game. She told him that she just wanted to sit and enjoy her drink, which, for some reason, enraged Lionel. Snapping to her, "I just ain't feeling this!" he walked out, leaving her alone in the bar, completely puzzled by his behavior, but completely relieved that she had finally seen the last of him.

Lionel walked away from his last three relationships.

Trying to explain his actions, Lionel pointed out that he was just too high-class for Martinique, making a particular point to mock her hair weave.

For her part, Martinique met someone interesting at the bar after Lionel left and said that she knew exactly who was too high-class for whom. And besides, it's a wig, not a weave.

Cameron and Gary

Now, on paper, Cameron and Gary seem like a fine match. Who would ever predict that their date—which began so pleasantly—would descend into the very lowest depths of blind date meltdown hell? But that's just what happened. This was the worst meltdown ever. No contest. It was the *China Syndrome* of blind dates. It was so bad it gave flashbacks to people in Chernobyl.

And yet it began with such promise. Cameron is a 25-year-old from Huntington Beach. Is she lively? According to her, she's the Energizer Bunny's sister (although DNA tests don't support her claim). Cameron says she's always happy and very athletic. And she's looking for a guy who's just like her. Except, well, a guy.

So Cameron was set up with Gary, a 26-year-old chef from San Diego who calls himself funny, daring, spontaneous, and cute. So far, so good, right? Wrong.

When they first met, she commented on the bag he carried. When he told her it was a Lakers bag, she said enthusiastically, "I *love* the Lakers." Gary replied, "You do, huh? We're gonna get along just fine then." This is the kind of line that, in a feature film, would be known as ironic foreshadowing.

In the car, Gary laid on the compliments like, "You're short, but you'll do." He related amusing stories about his past, like the time he ran "butt naked" through a fancy restaurant. He said that he did things like this because, "You only live once." Cameron replied that she didn't think that was true—she believes in reincarnation.

 Gary majored in finance but minored in booty.

Things deteriorated a little when they went to a park to play a rousing game of croquet. Well, perhaps rousing isn't the operative word. "Bitter," "angry"—those are words that characterize the game a little more precisely. Cameron cheated frequently, which made Gary angry. He repeatedly tried to cop a feel, which didn't do anything for Cameron's mood: "There's no butt touching on this date!" After she "won" her cheating game, Gary berated her. "I thought you was an independent 2000 woman." Cameron: "I am. I'm independently kickin' your butt." Gary: "You smell that? I smell bullcrap. You have a violent side, you need help." And on that note, it was off to a lovely dinner.

 Cameron could never handle her booze.

At the restaurant, Gary tried to get her to talk about sex, but Cameron concentrated on tossing back the drinks. In fact, she finally got so snookered that she actually went so far as to sing "How Dry I Am." Gary said, "Oh yeah, you're going to be a cartoon character by the end of the night." Then he turned the conversation back to sex. After a long silence, Cameron said, "You're a sicko. Is that all you men think about? Sex?" Gary replied, "Ninety-nine percent of the time, yeah."

After dinner, they decided to go play some pool, apparently having forgotten how much fun the croquet had been. In the cab, Gary made sure to tell Cameron that her breath stank of garlic and booze and that she should get a mint. For some reason, this made her angry. "Don't try to clown me," she said. "'Cause I can get ugly." More foreshadowing, but not ironic this time.

 Gary doesn't deal well with rejection.

The pool game turned out to be nothing more than an excuse for Gary to get some cheap feels. He asked her for a kiss. She said, "That's not allowed on the first date." He started to touch her backside and she cautioned, "If you smack my butt, you will lose me as a friend." Gary smirked and said, "Who said I wanted to be your friend? I just want dirty, sweat-hot sex."

And that is when it all began to unravel. Let's hear the rest in their own words.

CAMERON: "So, why did you just turn into a jerk like within five minutes?"
GARY: "'Cause I'm not having fun. You're boring."
CAMERON: "You're whack, dude."
GARY: "You're saying some of the stupidest stuff I've ever heard in my life. Dumb, air-headed."

 Nothing wins points like calling her stupid.

CAMERON: "It takes two to hold a conversation."

GARY: "The lack of brain cells involved in your . . . thought processes. Either you smoke too much or you didn't learn enough. One of the two. I can't stand it. *IT DOESN'T MATTER!* Come on, I'm outta here. Bye."

CAMERON: "What's your fat-ass problem?"

GARY: "My fat-ass problem? You got more belly than me!"

CAMERON: "I don't think so. Can we leave, please?"

GARY: "At least I don't have a hole in my lip, dropping all kind of wine on my shirt."

Therapist Joe Says:

Gary is frustrated and has gone on the attack.

CAMERON: "You need to shut the fuck up."

Cameron stormed out of the pool hall and Gary followed her to the sidewalk.

CAMERON: "Why were you acting like such a nice guy? Why were you acting? Why didn't you just be the asshole that you are?"

GARY: "I was not acting. I was trying to be cool."

CAMERON: "Why don't you be the jerk that you are?"

GARY: "I was trying to be cool but you not giving no love. I don't get no hug, no kiss, no nothin.'"

CAMERON: "You get that at the end of the day! You get the hug at the end of the day."

GARY: "I'm tired of it."

CAMERON: "Bye-bye."

GARY: "Oh, I'm sorry. You don't have a car. You're walkin'! I got a car. I'm out. Peace!"

CAMERON: "Ugly! Fat!"

GARY: "Man, look at you, you zit-prone woman! Oh my god!"

Zit-prone is rarely a compliment.

CAMERON: "Shut up, razor bump ass!"
GARY: "You probably got two double X chromosomes!"
CAMERON: "And you are dumb and bald!"
GARY: "You probably a hermaphrodite!"
CAMERON: "And you are dumb and bald!"
GARY: "Look, you probably got balls!"
CAMERON: "Don't make me get ugly! I'm outta here! Cut the camera! Cut!"

Of course, it goes without saying that any date that ends with the couple referring to each other as "zit-prone woman" and "razor-bump ass" is almost certainly not going to end in romance. In this case, it seems lucky things didn't end in bloodshed.

Gloria and Burt

There are many reasons that a blind date can melt down. Perhaps the two parties are simply incompatible and they get to a point where they can no longer bear the other's company. Perhaps a series of impossible-to-avoid events conspire to ruin the fun, causing tempers to flare and cutting the date short. But in this case, the reason is pretty clear: yep, that would be Gloria. As both she and her date Burt will have occasion to say during their date, she's evil.

Now Gloria didn't say she was evil at first. In fact, this 26-year-old social worker described herself as funny, intelligent, and easygoing. She said that she was looking for a man who's clean, funny, and good looking.

Well, Burt is certainly clean, reasonably good looking, and, if not funny exactly, at least he has a sunny and cheerful demeanor. At least he did until he met Gloria. Burt is a 33-year-old manager for a large chain of grocery stores who describes himself as outgoing, ambitious, and friendly.

He runs a 30 million dollar operation.

But "outgoing, ambitious, and friendly" just didn't cut it with Gloria. She took her first look at Burt and decided that he was way too white bread for her. Or rather, that she was just too magnificent for him. Burt, on the other hand, has no complaints about Gloria, thinking immediately that she was a looker of the highest order. In their initial conversation she said to him that she's just too nice—and wishes she wasn't. Little did Burt know that wishes like this can come true sooner than he might hope.

He sees the world through rose-colored glasses.

When Gloria learned that Burt was a grocery store manager, she immediately began to demean his profession, imagining him to be nothing more than a bagboy. At first she was joking—later, she was seriously mean.

Gloria feels superior when she belittles others.

They had a bit of fun at a costume shop, trying on crazy hats. Burt dressed like a pimp and Gloria put on a pink wig, which she wore for a great deal of the date.

Things remained nominally friendly until dinner when Burt, rather ill-advisedly, asked what she thought when she first saw him. Gloria replied, "You would make a very nice friend." He said he didn't believe they had much chemistry and Gloria said that she could make him believe they had chemistry if she wanted to.

BURT: "You're not that evil."
GLORIA: "I can be."

And it's true—she can be.

At dinner, defending himself against her growing barrage of insults, Burt told Gloria that she was way too high-maintenance and asked why she can't go for more than a minute or two without looking in the mirror (he was, perhaps, shocked that she actually cast a reflection). Gloria told Burt that she is completely out of his league. "Your friends wouldn't set you up with me because they'd go out with me first."

BURT: "You think you're all that and a bag of chips and you're not."
GLORIA: "You're just mad because I don't like you. I've never ever not gotten anything I've ever wanted in my entire life. Tomorrow I'll wake up to a beautiful life and you'll wake up to your life."

She mocked him again for working in a grocery store. When Burt pointed out that he was actually the manager of a grocery store, she replied, "You can't even manage your own wardrobe."

Even grocery store managers have their limit, and this appeared to be Burt's. He finally walked away, as she shouted after him, taunting him all the way, "Make sure you have a clean uniform for tomorrow at work!"

Burt rode home alone, which was probably the best company he had all day. In her post-date interview, Gloria said, "He's a chump. The only way we will go out again is if he is bagging my groceries." Burt just said the obvious: "She's evil."

Ask Therapist Joe

Therapist
Joe
Says:

In every episode of *Blind Date,* Therapist Joe offers an observation or two about the couples' behavior. Because he's so consistently on the money—and because the real-life Therapist Joe, Michael I. Gold, Ph.D., has more degrees than scalding water—visitors to the *Blind Date* web site have started writing in asking the good shrink for dating and relationship advice.

Maybe he addresses one of your problems somewhere in the following letters. If not, you can write to him yourself at the *Blind Date* website.

Q: Are men and women attracted to similar things in each other?
A: That is a great question. In national studies, women ranked intelligence number one in importance followed by humor second. This statistic was reversed in men, who ranked a sense of humor highest. You might be surprised to know that while men ranked intelligence second, looks were around fourth and fifth. Men seem to appreciate a sense of humor because it gives them a sense of inclusion and ac-

ceptance. Women ranked intelligence highest, as it replaces brute force as a characteristic of a provider in our culture. You realize of course that this makes Bill Gates one of the sexiest men in America.

Q: Does the guy always have to pay on the first date?
A: I think it depends on where you are going and who asked who out. An important factor is also who is more economically able to handle it. In our culture it is customary to equate money with the ability to protect. Money is power in our culture. Typically it is expected that the male display his "fitness" in dollar bills. Of course whenever I'm short of cash I try to impress my lady by bench-pressing the waiter.

Q: I am currently involved in a long distance relationship. I would like nothing more than for it to work; however I'm afraid the distance will tear us apart.
A: Long distance relationships can work, but they require effort. Although being apart seems strange, it is not rare. Many families must work around rigid schedules because of careers, school, and even the military. If you decide to come together, the one who moves will be leaving his entire social network behind. In order for it to truly work, both partners must concentrate on creating a new social network and independence for the partner who got uprooted. It isn't easy, but if you care enough, it's possible to make it work. Hey, and if it doesn't work out, there's always Russian mail-order brides.

Q: It seems like my boyfriend and I constantly argue. I know we love each other but lately it seems like everything erupts into a fight. Is there anything we can do?
A: This is a common question and a good one. Confrontation is generally a failure in communication. What people need to do is turn confrontation into curiosity so that an angry experience can become a learning experience. There are also arguments that can't be resolved. Next time an argu-

ment breaks out, see if you can ask questions to diffuse the situation. Like, "Honey, is the gun cabinet locked?"

Q: My girlfriend likes to play with sex toys. Is that healthy?
A: Many men are intimidated by sex toys because they believe that the woman will become "addicted" to their power and size. Indeed, the Kinsey Institute of Sexual Study shows that there is some truth to this. However, most women who are used to a vibrator for gratification can, after a short period of time, be satisfied with the good old-fashioned penis. Bottom line, there is nothing to fear. Have as much fun as you can and please your partner as much as possible. People are far more sexually adaptable than we give them credit for.

Q: My boyfriend and I are constantly fighting over money issues. I am aware of the power of money issues in a relationship and want to avoid this conflict. Any ideas?
A: Money isn't only the root of all evil, it's the number one cause of divorce in this country. Money represents both time and power. In a capitalist society, the one with the most money is seen as being better than his neighbors. Money produces competitive feelings between people. Being aware of these money issues when you are discussing finances could be helpful in easing the situation. You may also want to just simplify the whole thing by become enormously wealthy.

Q: I am getting over a recent divorce and would like to begin dating again. I am worried about how this will affect my relationship with my daughter. I love her so much, but I need some companionship. What can I do?
A: Well, first, don't feel lonely—you share one of the fastest growing problems in our culture. There is a lack of support for single parents looking to start dating again. You have every right to go out and enjoy yourself. Just make sure that you take all the necessary precautions before you do—especially

hiring a baby-sitter that your child is familiar with. Let your daughter know that you will not be far away and will be home close to a specific time. This is not a situation in which you should ask your child's permission. You should do this for you. Just make sure she is taken care of. Also, I would recommend that, within the boundaries of safety, initial sexual contact not take place in your own home. Other than that, have a great time. And good luck—judging from what I've seen on our show, I think you'll need it.

Q: I am planning on getting a boob job. Is there any risk in going big?
A: I support people's wishes to look as attractive as they can. With the availability of cosmetic surgery, many people are able to overcome easily any feelings of inadequacy. The philosophy of going all the way may be problematic. I would check out chat rooms and talk to professional physicians to find out what problems occur from breast augmentation. A common side effect to the operation is a loss of sensation. Large breasts, although appealing to me, can result in all kinds of problems, from inappropriate advances to severe back pain. Good luck. In the meantime, please send in before and after pictures—for clinical purpose only, of course.

Q: Why does it seem that some guys are turned off by a forward woman?
A: Males traditionally believe that it's their place to ask the woman out. The hunter does not want to give up his role and become the hunted. It's sad to me that so many women who express their feelings are seen as being forward or pushy. Women do run the risk of being perceived negatively when initiating contact, but I feel that they should express themselves and tell the guys to get over it. That caveman stuff doesn't cut it anymore. The revolution is now, sister!

Q: I was out with a few of my guy friends the other night and they were trying to tell me that any woman could have any guy in the place. As a woman, I know better. Where would they get that idea?

A: As I just said, a woman who is forward can be perceived as being "easy." Men often perceive sex as a commitment of only minutes while women know that the consequences can last much longer. Women are therefore more likely to regard more seriously the decision to have sex. Men see this difference as giving women all the power to initiate sex. This is silly because everyone knows that sex comes about through a combination of Hai Karate cologne and Tom Jones music.

Q: Lately I have not been having the best luck attracting the opposite sex. Do you have any advice for a guy who's a bit down on his luck?

A: Ah, the age-old question: how do I get the girls to like me? Well, here are some ideas. Expand your interests, and people will expand their interests in you. People are most often physically attracted to people who are interesting. The key to being an interesting person is to be interested. Involving yourself in a social setting such as an acting class, a sports team, or yoga is the first step to an enriched life. This is the best way to find someone and to be happy with yourself. Of course you could do like many of the writers on *Blind Date* and just give up altogether.

Q: I have a friend who I feel is being played by this guy she's seeing. Whenever they go out, she always pays, but I know this guy's not even into her. Should I say something?

A: It is very difficult for someone to hear that they are in a relationship which others perceive as a poor one. Your friend may think that even a bad relationship is better than none at all. She also may feel that paying for everything is her way of maintaining control. Very often if you try to confront someone in a situation like this, they will deny or rationalize the truth. I'd say be a good friend and have the pint of Häagen-Daz ready for when she comes to her senses.

Q: Why do so many women say they'd like to be "just friends" at the end of an evening?

A: If a woman tells you she'd like to be "just friends" she has just told you that she doesn't find you sexually attractive. It is my belief that working to change her perception is futile because it is typically based on "chemistry," that mysterious phenomenon that occurs between two people leading to romance. Chemistry is either there or it isn't. My suggestion as a fellow man is to learn to take the "just friends" blow with style. Crying and clinging to her leg as she leaves the restaurant only makes things worse. Believe me, I know . . . I mean I've read about it.

Q: Lately I have found myself having a crush on this guy at work. I am involved in a serious relationship that I would not want to jeopardize. Is it possible to be in love with someone while having a crush on someone else?

A: I think that it is possible not only to have a crush on someone but to be in love with different people at the same time. Human beings, as a species, seem to have trouble with monogamy. Well over 60 percent of both males and females have reported having extramarital sexual encounters. But acting on a feeling is different than just having a fantasy. As an example, while making love with your boyfriend, fantasizing about being with someone else or somewhere else is common. Turning that fantasy into an action can and usually does result in trouble. There is no peach without a pit—well, with the exception of those new genetically engineered peaches, but that's another question for another time.

Q: I have recently found myself in a situation where I am choosing between two different guys. The one I'd most like to be with lives about an hour and a half away while the other lives just around the block. Not having a lot of faith in long distance relationships, I am thinking of settling for convenience rather than passion.

A: It is okay to date someone for any reason. Just because you date someone doesn't mean you'll be with them forever. Dating is the process of finding the qualities you both like and dislike in others. With a divorce rate of 60 percent in this country, it's easy to see that many relationships are not forever. It's actually okay to have a second-class relationship. It is not okay, however, to pretend that a second-class relationship is true love . . . unless it is with a member of 'N Sync. In that case, go for the gold—they're dreamy!

Q: I have heard different things on this matter so I thought I'd ask the pro. What is better, boxers or briefs?
A: This is a situation where comfort is the key consideration. However, during times of conception, the male would be advised to wear loose-fitting clothes. This prevents restricting the sperm and slowing their movement, which can be detrimental to pregnancy. Tight-fitting jeans have also been known to have a negative effect on conception. That's ironic, since tight jeans can often be the cause of attempting contraception. Hey, I say when all else fails, try going commando.

Q: Why does that initial feeling of love wear off? Where does the fire go?
A: The initial feeling of love is literally a chemical reaction that takes place in your brain. I believe that this exists in the name of procreation, not cohabitation. The initial period of lust leads many people to find that the most erotic experiences in their lives were also the most neurotic. As a relationship matures, the couple is less affected by these chemicals. Somewhere along the way this leads to your dad lying around the house in black socks and boxers.

Q: I have been seeing this woman for two years now. How can you tell if someone is marriage material?
A: Well, if you have to ask if she's the marrying type after two years of being together, she probably isn't. You should al-

ready know the answer. The first few months of a relationship act as an interview period through which each partner discovers the other's intentions towards goals, timelines, and the future. Individuals should have these decisions made before they begin to share a life with another. People need to pick a path before they pick a person.

Q: I seem to always be attracted to the same type of guy. Is there a right type for everyone? What are people attracted to in someone else?
A: Attraction can often be traced to an unconscious level. We are generally attracted to people as a way to work out unresolved issues from our childhood. We tend to "fall" for the same type of person over and over because we all seek out what is familiar. It would be extremely rare for a person normally attracted to slender, tall people to become attracted to a short, overweight person. Some of this is due to our hard-wiring and some is due to our past successes and failures with people of certain types.

Q: Are there any tricks to making sure your relationship is long and healthy?
A: I believe the things that keep people together are flexibility, curiosity, nondefensiveness, humor, and compatible values. It is important to know the roots of any disagreements and conflict. Money is the biggest issue in all broken marriages. Learn how to deal with conflict. The majority of confrontations evolve from miscommunication.

Q: I have recently started seeing someone new. I am quickly falling into my old poor dating habits. I want to keep my individuality but still be part of a healthy relationship. How do I balance this?
A: Many people have problems establishing boundaries in their relationships. Everyone has both the need to belong and the need to be alone. Understanding this is the key to mastering your problem. Remember, all relationships end in

separation, even "till death do us part" ones. Take things slow and enjoy the beginnings of an exciting new partnership. Or forget dating altogether and take up a hobby. I collect Captain and Tennille memorabilia—it's fun!

Q: My girlfriend is obsessed with sex in public. Everywhere we go she's trying to get us in trouble. Is this healthy?
A: The question is more about legality than health. Your girlfriend seems to be an exhibitionist. This is common in a society where those values are repressed. From clothing to sexual behavior, exhibitionism is something that our society unconsciously encourages. From a psychological view, most exhibitionists are latent voyeurs. Their sexual charge comes from imagining what they look like to other people. And when it comes to sex, danger—as in getting caught—has always been a turn-on. But, you know, you don't have to go out to find danger—you could always try running with scissors.

Q: I watch *Blind Date* and often you will have women who enjoy getting their toes sucked. Is there really such a thing as a foot fetish and what does it mean?
A: Fetishes are things that a person focuses on which causes them to feel erotic. One of the most common of them all, cross-culturally, is the foot fetish. The general psychological take on this fetish is that the person involved is playing hero or goddess fantasies. Kissing someone's feet is one of the oldest forms of submission in human culture. It's right up there with relinquishing control of the remote.

Q: Why do men always say they'll call and never do?
A: Why does it seem like I'm always having to defend my gender? The next time this happens to you, try not to get too upset. It's just a man's way of protecting you. To sound like a *National Geographic* special, the male of the species feels as if it is his position to protect the female from harm. A man thinks that by not calling, it will somehow ease the blow. In reality, he is skirting the issue of confrontation while avoiding

having to see the hurt he is inflicting on a woman. Although I agree that dignity is sometimes better than confrontation, it is possible that a man in this situation will end up doing more harm than good.

Q: How can I be sure that I am the best in bed that I can be? How can I be better?
A: The most important steps toward pleasing your lover are: ask, listen, and explore. These are things you should be doing when you are with your lover. Ask if she is being fulfilled and if there is anything she'd like for you to do. Listen to her. She may be giving you both subtle and not so subtle clues when things feel good. Explore. Take time to learn each other's bodies. Be comfortable with your partner. The best sex is when you can enjoy each other.

Q: I have been seeing this woman for a few months now, and I have genuine feelings for her. I want to know, is it ever too soon for sex? How long should couples wait?
A: Well this is one of those "it depends" kind of questions. First off, some people have certain beliefs which prevent them from consummating a relationship until they are married. If that is not the case, take your cues from your lover. Try hinting and testing the water. It is always a good idea to talk openly about the subject with your partner to make her feel comfortable. You should state your intentions and see how she reacts. Remember, it is always a decision that must be made mutually. A word of caution: there are many treatable and nontreatable sexually transmitted diseases. When you are sleeping with someone, you are sleeping with everyone they have been with before you. It is unfortunate that making love has become so dangerous, but it is necessary to be the guardian of your and your lover's health.

Q: I have been out with this girl a few times now, yet I am not sure how she feels about me. Are there any signs that I could look to as hints to how she feels about me?

A: There have been many books written on the subject of nonverbal communication. My favorite is Desmond Morris's *The Human Animal.* Nonverbal cues change from culture to culture. In general, if a person is open with his body, arms and legs *not* crossed, he is open to receiving you. Mild contact is a sign of inviting more intimate touching. It is also a good way for you to feel out the situation. Another clue to look for: if a person is touching his nose a lot, he may be lying to you. Polite staring with a smile is the single most common cross-cultural signal. I wonder if flipping the bird is a close second.

Q: What is the deal with women and flowers? They can never get enough.
A: First off, let's not be sexist here. Men love flowers too. Flowers and other such gifts represent fragrance, color, and nature. There happens to be a massive marketing campaign around gift-giving in general. Flowers have been marked as the universal gift to give women on any occasion. Including the time you agreed maybe her pants may have been too tight, or the time you complained that her tuna casserole tasted like motor oil.

Q: Do you believe in love at first sight?
A: Absolutely, however . . . be sure to take a second look. When a person is attractive to us, all kinds of chemicals are released in our brain. This is known as falling in love. If we are interested in a long-term relationship with someone, it is the person's character, not looks, that we need to become in love with. Falling in love can be an extremely powerful narcotic and has made many people do many foolish things. Just look at Tommy Lee and Pamela.

Q: Does size matter?
A: The answer to that question is both yes and no. Women on average only possess nerve endings for the initial two inches of the vaginal barrel. The full length of the vaginal bar-

rel is only four inches long, from opening to cervix. The average width is ¾ of an inch. The average male is 3½ inches to 6 inches when erect. So while it is medically possible to not satisfy your mate, it is mathematically rare. Trust me—there are so many other ways to disappoint your lover that I wouldn't even worry about this one.

Q: I'm thinking about making a move on a coworker. Is it wrong to mix business with pleasure?

A: I feel that office flirting is okay as long as you are both aware of what you want from each other. It can be hard enough to navigate through relationships without having to see the other person every day. One false move with these types of interactions could make your workday even longer than it already seems. Be cautious but have fun, enjoy, and use the mistletoe to your advantage.

Q: I have heard that in order to preserve your spirit and energy you should refrain from completing the act of sex. Is that true?

A: Remember the scene in the movie *Rocky* where his manager tells him to stay away from women 'cause they "ruin the legs?" Well, he was referring to what you are asking about. While it's not proven that sperm count has an effect on performance, it is a widely held superstition that preserving your "cowboys" will harness your energy. Many athletes refrain from sex before a big game and some artists abstain to increase creativity. Of course there is a downside. Refraining from sex can result in chewed ice, ground teeth, broken pencils, crushed soda cans, walking into walls, crying . . . etc.

Q: My boyfriend is always pressuring me into sex. He says that it is not medically safe to deny him. Is it possible to get hurt from not having sex?

A: Having sex should always be your choice. Never let anyone persuade you into doing it. If you want your boyfriend to know the truth tell him that sperm is stored in the epididimus for 72 hours before it is absorbed into the body. There is no harm in abstaining from sex. Next time he's pressuring you into bed give him a Rubik's cube; that will take his mind off it for a while.

Q: Since you work on a dating show, I was hoping you could give me a great first date idea.

A: Sure. I highly recommend that a first date activity take place during the day. Good activities are ones in which two people can share an event and talk to one another at the same time. Sporting events lend themselves to this behavior so that the focus can transfer back and forth from the event to the couple. Movies are not the greatest idea for a first date, especially ones at the Pussycat Theatre.

▼▼▼▼▼▼▼▼▼▼▼▼▼   ▼▼▼▼▼▼▼▼▼▼▼▼▼

Behind the Scenes
at Blind Date with
The Blind Date Answer Guy

Some people watch *Blind Date* and are entertained. Some people watch *Blind Date* and scream with laughter. Some people watch *Blind Date* and are horrified. Some people watch *Blind Date* and thank their lucky stars that they are married or in prison and out of the dating scene. And some people watch *Blind Date* and wonder.

What do they wonder? They wonder lots of things. And when they wonder, they do the logical thing: they ask the *Blind Date* Answer Guy.

And what do they ask, you ask? Well, viewers have questions about all kinds of things—the technical aspects of the show or the personalities of the daters or what happened to that couple after their date or just exactly who Obvious Guy is and why irony continues to elude him. They especially wonder just why everyone who appears on the show apparently owns the same Ford Explorer.

Well, the answers to all those questions, both niggling and profound, are to be found in the following pages. We have gathered all the queries that have come in over the *Blind Date* transom and, frankly, made up others so that you can get the full poop on exactly how the show is produced. This is your peek behind the scenes, as it were. It's the next best thing to actually visiting the palatial and lavish *Blind Date* offices in Hollywood where glamour, eroticism, and comedic brilliance suffuse every luxurious office and where even the day-old bagels taste like pure gold.

In coming up with the answers to these questions, the *Blind Date* Answer Guy observes the age-old tradition of all great journalists and their dogs, giving you the 411 on the "Six W's": who, what, when, where, why, and woof.

So read on. You're about to get your Ph.D. in *Blind Date*–ology. And remember, there are no stupid questions. Just questions asked by stupid people.

Where do you find your contestants for the show?

The contestants come from everywhere, from Zanzibar to Barkeley Square, from the Panhandle of Texas to the rockbound coasts of Maine. And, occasionally, from Chicago. Sometimes *Blind Date* finds the daters, sometimes the daters find *Blind Date.* Did you ever notice how many singles on the show describe themselves as "the life of the party" or "uninhibited" or "wild"? That's because those are precisely the kind of folks who catch the attention of the show's recruiters and, they hope, will also capture the attention of the home viewer, which is, of course, you.

These *Blind Date* field recruiters scour clubs, bars, restaurants, and other popular hot spots in Los Angeles and other major cities searching for exciting, attractive individuals who might want to take a chance with a blind date. The recruiters usually hone in on the people who seem to be the center of attention in their groups. Outgoing individuals whose personalities stand out usually make great dates for the show. The only trouble is if they're *really* outstanding at a club and truly going over the top, sometimes they don't really remember the next day that they were approached by *Blind Date* at all. But if they do, they call up to make an appointment to come in and be interviewed.

But, just as often, people call the number at the end of each episode or log onto the website and contact the show themselves.

Well then, if you know so much, what is the casting process like?

Potential contestants are brought into the *Blind Date* offices for an interview. This is a little like taking the SATs, except with much hotter clothes. But trust us: plenty of people who miserably failed the SATs make out like gangbusters on this particular exam. Let's just say it's a test that requires little or no brainpower, but plenty of personality and a certain degree of fearlessness.

First, the hopeful singles fill out a comprehensive questionnaire that asks them everything from the basics—name, age, hair color—to more provocative questions about turn-ons and turn-offs, most embarrassing experiences, one-night stands, and qualities that they look for in a member of the opposite sex. Then, they're brought into the *Blind Date* "confessional" for a videotaped interview. Here they can tell the camera a little about themselves, maybe describe some interesting dating moments from the past, or describe a dating fantasy that they hope might be fulfilled on the show. The clips of each dater that are shown before each date are culled from these longer interviews. Each applicant is encouraged to speak freely in talking about personality, experience, fantasies, and other intimate subjects. And sometimes they speak very freely indeed. Yikes.

After this process is completed, the show's casting office goes over each questionnaire and interview and picks the most compelling personalities. Then they go about matching each single up with an appropriate mate. This is the tricky part, of course. It won't be until the night of the actual date that they learn whether their match worked or not.

How many dates do you shoot?

Lots and lots and lots. *Blind Date* is a strip show. That doesn't mean it's a program on which people strip—although, certainly, that happens now and then, and the producers are delighted when it does. No, in this case, "strip show" means that the program airs six days a week. Since every show consists of two dates, this means that literally hundreds of dates must be taped for each season. The work is divided among three crews, each consisting of a field producer, a cameraman, a soundman, a grip, and, of course, the psychic who reads the daters' minds for the thought bubbles. The grip, on the other hand, rarely reads anything; he or she is responsible for lighting the scenes and smoothing out the overall production, which is a very important job. All three crews work nearly every day and night of the week in order to fill the huge order for dates. Basically, *Blind Date* is produced by a lot of very tired people.

How long is each date?

When they air on the show each date lasts about six minutes. In reality, the dates are much longer. About ten minutes.

Kidding.

Actually, the aim is to try and keep the couples together for about eight hours. Now, that's longer than most first dates would normally last, but it's done that way for a reason. Eight hours or so is long enough to capture enough footage and visit all the different locations, and short enough for the daters to avoid becoming bored with the date and with each other. Or with the grip.

Let's break it down. The typical date goes like this: one single picks up the other at his or her home. They then get into the van to drive to their first activity. Sometimes this first drive can be forty-five minutes or an hour long, giving them plenty of time to chat and begin to get to know each other. They then arrive at the first location, which usually involves doing something active, like playing catch on the beach, or Rollerblading or shooting elk. Come on, they don't really shoot elk. Stay with me here.

Then they drive to another activity. This can be a long drive, too, allowing for more of that valuable getting-to-know-you time. The next activity might be some kind of project such as painting a picture or building a model or shooting an elk. Gotcha again. Pay attention.

At about this time, usually they change into fancier duds and head off for dinner. This is where the romantic stuff can start to happen. Or, conversely, it's when one of the daters decides that she hates the way the other one slurps his pasta and the melt-down begins. Either way, it's good TV.

After dinner, it's back to the van and on to the next location of the evening. Usually, this is a bar, coffee shop, or ice cream parlor. And this, depending on how things are going, will either lead home or, as happens about 80 percent of the time, to the Jacuzzi. Then they drive home, which could be another long trip.

See? All that adds up to a long time. An even longer time than it took to answer this question. But it's necessary in order to get a date that's filled with visual interest as well as intriguing personalities. Or, to put it another way, if you can't do the time, don't do the crime. The daters are advised that they should expect to be with the *Blind Date* crews for a full ten hours. Even more, if one of the locations is in the South Seas.

Why does everyone on the show drive a Ford Expedition?

The more important question is, why wouldn't they? The Expedition is a fine vehicle for a *Blind Date*—it's roomy enough for comfort and has all four tires so important for forward motion. However, obviously, all those Expeditions don't belong to the daters—they belong to the show. *Blind Date* owns three Ford Expeditions, each of which is equipped with three cameras. Two minicams (or, as they're known in the biz, "lipstick cams") are mounted on the windshield and point back at each dater. The third camera is manned by a crew member riding snugly in the rear of the vehicle. Any time the daters enjoy a beverage of the alcoholic kind—even one drink—they can no longer drive themselves. They must get into a cab and be driven around. At that point, the couple sits in the backseat and the third camera moves to the front seat to catch every fascinating word and gesture. And if it seems that every cab is driven by the same man, and that every single location can only be reached by passing Los Angeles' El Rey Theater, then you must be seeing things. So snap out of it.

I really love those great thought bubbles. But how do you know what people are thinking?

One of *Blind Date*'s most fiercely guarded secrets is the constant presence of Swami Boutros-Boutros Jenkins, a mind reader and licensed aromatherapist who accompanies every couple on every date. The swami spends a few moments with each of our singles before the date begins in order to create a mind meld, and if you've seen some of our singles, you know what a trick that can be. Then he sits just behind them when they're in the van or cab, or under the table when they're at restaurants and bars, and scribbles furiously at every moment, writing down each thought that enters their heads. Of course, some dates require substantially less writing than others, but that goes without saying. The swami's greatest challenge is, of course, the frequent trips to the Jacuzzi that are a hallmark of *Blind Date*. He has been known to remain submerged for hours at a time, causing enormous problems not only for his breathing but for his legal pad. Sometimes, after a particularly lengthy session in the hot tub, the swami resembles nothing so much as a giant pitted prune wearing a sopping wet turban. When dry, he looks more like a bulk order of beef jerky, except with more gold teeth. Though avidly courted by other television shows such as *60 Minutes* and *Bowlin' For Big Bucks!*, Swami Boutros-Boutros Jenkins works exclusively for *Blind Date*. On days when no dates are being taped, he hangs around the office, helping the producers find their keys.

Who determines where they go on their date?

On the original questionnaire that each dater fills out on the day of their first interview, the applicants are asked where they'd like to go on a date. Some of them suggest a movie or perhaps a nice play—either of which would really make compelling television, wouldn't it? And some suggest having dinner in Paris. Now, that's just ridiculous. Nobody on *Blind Date* has dinner in Paris except the executive producers. The more realistic applicants suggest activities like volleyball, bicycling, and surfing. And, for some reason, they all want to go to very, very expensive restaurants, once they learn the show is picking up the tab. After the applicant is selected to appear on the show, his or her questionnaire is passed on to another department where segment producers work to plan activities similar to their requests, if possible. The idea is to try to accommodate a dater's interests as well as provide activities promoting communication between the couple. Sometimes, of course, the activities are chosen simply to put the couple in a peculiar situation, just to see how it affects their developing relationship. And sometimes nobody has any ideas at all, which is how couples sometimes end up in the park playing checkers or something. I mean, *checkers!* Sheesh.

Oddly enough, almost no one ever asks to go to the hot tub and yet so very, very many of them end up there. Coincidence? Perhaps, perhaps not.

What is the number of dates you shoot compared to ones you actually show?

"Waste not, want not" is the watchword at *Blind Date*. (Another one, for some reason, is "A watched pot never boils." Which is patently ridiculous, because it does, eventually.) Because this is so-called "reality" TV, *Blind Date* can use almost every date shot. For the purposes of the show, it doesn't matter much whether the date goes very well or very badly. Either way, the producers can distill an entertaining six-minute essence from it. On *Blind Date* the only sin is boredom—but even boring dates can be magically transformed into comic masterpieces by a well-placed caption or thought bubble or graphic. (Check the sidebar on "Most Boring Blind Date" on page 123 for a good example of how things can sometimes go kerflooey.)

The only time in the history of the show that a date hasn't aired is because of equipment malfunctions or location difficulties. And even those occasions have come along only two or three times out of several hundred dates shot.

It seems as if a majority of the dates don't work out. Do you set them up to fail?

Most blind dates in so-called "real life" don't work out all that well, either. An enterprise like this is a real roll of the dice. Think about it—you've probably set up two friends that you just know will be perfect for each other and they end up getting along about as well as Godzilla and Megalon. Not your fault—and not their fault, either. Just works out that way. All *Blind Date* casting has to go on are the questionnaires and the "confessional" interviews. And, you'll be shocked to learn, people sometimes present themselves differently at an interview than they do when actually on the job. One reason for making the date last so long is that, in most cases, the daters gradually become less aware of the camera and, eventually, their true characters emerge. And that can be good or bad. If you look at the thing from a statistical point of view, you'll find that the great majority of the show's dates are more in the middle range—they didn't love each other, they didn't hate each other. True hateful meltdowns are almost as rare as true love connections. But, of course, they're much funnier.

Okay, Mr. Statistics, how many dates actually *do* work out?

We've found that about 30 percent of the couples have had some kind of positive connection. Considering the circumstances under which they're meeting, and the constant pressure of a blind date of any kind, that really seems pretty good. In terms of lasting relationships, there have been two or three couples who are still together months, or even a couple of years, after their blind date. We're still waiting for our first *Blind Date* marriage—but we know it's coming along one of these days. At least we really, really hope so. Especially the *Blind Date* Answer Guy, who loves cake.

What is the time frame between when a date is first shot to when it's aired?

The turnaround time for a date is about three months. As with the date itself, there are many stages and steps that the post-production crew must go through before it gets to television screens across this great country of ours. Once a date is shot, it must first be broken down into a story. Segment producers watch every minute of each date, making notes about interesting activities and conversations, and slowly discovering what the essential story of the date is. This step alone can take quite a while when you consider that for each six-minute date that airs on TV, there are about eight hours worth of footage not shown.

Once the segment producers have completed what is called a "bin cut"—about a half-hour long condensation of the date—it moves up to a senior segment producer, which is basically like a segment producer except that they drive better cars. The senior segment producer hones the bin cut down to a razor-sharp eight or ten minutes, creating the captions, thought bubbles, and other patented *Blind Date* accoutrements, if you'll pardon my French.

At this point, the editors and graphic designers move in. Working with the senior segment producers, they create all the visual aids to the story and hone it down to a tight six minutes. They also add sound effects and choose appropriate music from the vast library created by *Blind Date*'s musical genius, Devin Powers.

Once the date has been completed, it is paired with another. Host Roger Lodge reviews the dates and then goes into the studio to shoot the "host wraps"—his introductions and comments which will air throughout the program. Only after these segments have been edited into the mix can the show be considered complete. And then, it's time to start all over again.

Who's the most famous person who ever appeared on the show?

Well, I guess it depends on your definition of "famous." Los Angeles radio personality Ryan Seacrest was on *Blind Date* in its first season. So was Jerri, who later went on to be one of the most hated members of the *Survivor II* cast in Australia. In the second season, Dirk, from the first *Survivor* cast, had a date that didn't go all that well—although he was so focused on himself that he didn't seem to notice. And then we matched up that *Temptation Island* temptress Lola with an unsuspecting single guy. Did he get tempted? Whoa yeah. Oh, and a *Blind Date* crew stumbled upon Fred Savage in a restaurant once, but he wouldn't sign a release, so he didn't actually make it to the show. Does that count?

Anyhoo, speaking of Roger Lodge–pretty good guy, is he?

He's a prince. Roger Lodge is, of course, the host of *Blind*

Date. It's his job to introduce the couples at the beginning, when hope still fills the air, and then offer a commentary on just how things went, once all the smoke has cleared. He first came to the attention of television viewers in 1995 while serving as a guest host on E! Entertainment's *Talk Soup,* an Emmy Award-winning program that pokes fun of talk shows and reality shows (and which currently, you'll be glad to know, makes fun of *Blind Date*). This is where he also came to the attention of *Blind Date*'s producers, who recognized that Roger Lodge had the perfect combination of wit and likeability—along with a certain smart-aleck edge—that would be perfect for their new show.

As an actor, he has also appeared in hit TV shows like *The Parkers* and *Sabrina the Teenage Witch* and in feature films such as *Not of This Earth* and *The Fan,* starring Robert De Niro, which ain't too shabby.

Actually, becoming an actor and talk show host were Lodge's ambitions even when he was a kid growing up in southern California. But he had another ambition, too—he wanted to be a professional basketball player. He never exactly made it to the NBA, but he does play in an entertainment league. And he is indeed a champion when it comes to sports knowledge. Even the *Blind Date* Answer Guy, who knows all, sees all, can't hold a candle to Mr. Lodge when it comes to sports trivia—the guy knows everything. In fact, his sports expertise has even led him to appear on both ESPN and Fox Sports Net.

But here's the important thing about Roger Lodge and *Blind Date*: many television hosts just show up, read the cue-cards and go home. But that's not the way Lodge does things. He takes an active role in writing every host script, rewriting and reshaping the lines until they're just the way he wants them. That's one of the reasons why he has become so popular on the show—he's really expressing his own point of view in his own words.

However, according to Roger Lodge, introducing and commenting on the dates is one thing; going on them is quite another. "I don't have the cojones to go on a blind date," he once said. "And throwing a camera crew into the mix? Forget it!"

What's the deal with Therapist Joe? He seems to know everything.

Oh, indeed he does. You would, too, if you had a background like this guy. Well, not you personally, but you know what I mean.

Actually, before we discuss the good doctor, we should mention some of the other regular *Blind Date* characters who pop up from time to time to put their two cents' worth in about what's happening on the date. Their names pretty much tell the whole story on the kind of input they make. Let's see, there's Sarcastic Sid, Betty Etiquette, Frat Guy Freddy, Dr. Date, and Obvious Guy, along with a few other one-shot wonders.

But Therapist Joe is not like any of the others. He's a real, living, breathing human for starters. And, as I said earlier, a real smart guy. Like, hella smart. And his real name is neither Therapist nor Joe. In fact, he is Michael I. Gold, Ph.D.

Dr. Gold earned his doctorate in clinical psychology from Columbia Pacific University, and holds a whole slew of other degrees from UCLA and Cal State Northridge. He's a licensed marriage, family, and child therapist and is certified as both a sexual therapist and a hypnotherapist. Dr. Gold has taught at the college level, has served as a high school principal, and has had a successful private practice in psychotherapy for over thirty years.

In his spare time, Dr. Gold is a certified SCUBA diver/instructor, a trapshooter, a close-up magician, and an avid collector of historical and cultural documents. And he is definitely the only person on the *Blind Date* staff who is a member of the American Psychological Association, the American Civil Liberties Union, the Society for the Magical Arts, and the Screen Actor's Guild, among many other organizations.

Do you hate this guy yet? Well, hold on. His list of achievements just keeps a-growing. He has served as a consultant on television shows like *M*A*S*H, Cheers, Frasier,* and *St. Elsewhere* and on motion pictures including *Nothing in Common, Bad Dreams,* and *Single White Female.* And he's a gaming/hotel consultant for Harrah's International, Caesar's Palace, and the Reno-Tahoe Chamber of Commerce. And that, my friends, is about a quarter of his actual résumé. It's exhausting just to contemplate.

So, that's who Therapist Joe is. But what does he do on *Blind Date*?

I was getting to that. Jeez. Dr. Gold comes to the lavish *Blind Date* production offices once a week. While there, he views each date that is currently being worked on and consults with the senior segment producers who are helping to shape the story. Whereas the fictional characters like Sarcastic Sid mostly pop up for purposes of getting a laugh, Therapist Joe's contribution is to offer some real insight into the character or behavior of the singles on the show. "Therapist Joe Says . . ." is almost never used as a joke. Of course, in the meantime, his cartoon image has become a kind of mascot for the show. When Therapist Joe isn't saying anything of a therapeutic nature, he can often be found hovering around in the background somewhere, surfing, bowling, or joining in any other kind of activity of the moment.

For the record, Dr. Michael Gold doesn't look anything like Therapist Joe. Many who know him compare him to a young Pierce Brosnan, although there are also those who believe that he bears an uncanny resemblance to *The Beverly Hillbillies'* Nancy Culp.

Whatever. So where does all that cool music come from? I dig those groovy sounds, man!

Hey buddy, Woodstock's over. Enough with the groovy. But you do pose a compelling question. As pointed out earlier, the music is composed, produced, and performed by Devin Powers. And before you ask, here's a little about him. He's a native of San Francisco, a singer, songwriter, and a master of just about any musical instrument you can mention. Powers' band, Cats:Choir, attracted a large and loyal West Coast following in the nineties and their album, *House:of:Dog,* was an enormous hit all over Europe.

The success of Cats:Choir led Powers to tour and record with rock legends like John Entwistle of the Who and Lee Rocker of the Stray Cats. In 1997, Devin and his band the Vents signed, along with Blink 182, to MCA records through indie label Cargo. The Vents' national tour was highly successful and Powers was courted by executives from Universal Film and Television, who hired him as the music composer and supervisor for *Blind Date.* Literally every piece of music heard on the show was composed by Devin Powers, including the show's memorable theme song. To date, he has built a library of over three thousand musical pieces for the show, suitable for virtually any situation that might come up on a blind date. Occasionally the producers call on him to compose something specifically for an episode—they know that he can produce something remarkable even under a very tight deadline. And, in addition to writing the music, Powers plays all the instruments on the *Blind Date* tracks—he's truly a Renaissance man.

Devin Powers' work doesn't stop with *Blind Date.* His music can also be heard on such hit network shows as *Ed, Providence, Freakylinks, Chains of Love,* and *Fifth Wheel.* And he wrote the theme song to *The Living Century,* a television special produced by Barbra Streisand.

Okay, back to the show. Do any of the couples get along, you know, really *really* well?

Whoa yeah. Trust me on this one. Whew!

Now, you've seen some pretty racy stuff on the show. But usually not *too* racy. That's because *Blind Date* is syndicated. This means that different channels around the country can and do air it at different times in different cities. It might play at midnight in one town and at two in the afternoon somewhere else. Because of this, the producers are always careful to keep things within a certain standard of decency.

But people are people. Naturally, in the course of human events, things happen. There have been images of nudity or steamy passion caught on videotape by the *Blind Date* crews that are simply too compellingly erotic—one might even say explosively sexy—to ever be aired on TV, except possibly in Germany. While such moments are carefully trimmed from the broadcast episodes of *Blind Date* and while we cannot go into any details in what is, after all, a family-friendly book, rest assured that the author studied these scenes again and again and again just so he would be totally aware of what shouldn't be written here.

How can I get to be on *Blind Date*?

Well, it's pretty easy to contact the show. Just go to the web and head for the home page of *Blind Date* and click on "Sign up for *Blind Date*." Fill out the online questionnaire and send it in. If the perceptive folks in casting believe that you have the right stuff, they'll call you in for an interview. Be forewarned, however, that many are called, but few chosen. Many, many more singles apply for the show than actually get on. But just think what would happen if you actually made it. You might spend eight hours in a kind of living hell with an annoying date that otherwise you wouldn't cross the street to spit on. Or you might find the love of your life—the perfect dream mate. Hey, either way, it's bound to be interesting. And no matter what happens to you, your adventure will provide at least six minutes of laughs and cringes for the millions of *Blind Date* fans who will watch it. So give it a try—what have you got to lose?

The Wrap-Up

All right, so what have we learned here?

If you've actually been reading this book, as opposed to using it as a coaster, flyswatter, or gag gift, you've been able to pick up some valuable pointers on what to do—and not to do—not only on a blind date, but on a date of any kind. You've learned important lessons on bringing flowers—or flour—to your date; making interesting and marginally loony conversation in your first car ride; enjoying activities with a minimum of agony or humiliation; and determining whether your date is regarding you with love, lust, or loathing. You've learned how to intrigue—or, depending on which date you read about, how to enrage—a member of the opposite sex. You've learned how to murmur words of seduction and how to hurl insults. You've learned when your date is looking for long-term romance, or a one night stand.

Hundreds of daters, unsuspecting and otherwise, have sacrificed themselves on the altar of *Blind Date* in order for you to gain this wisdom, so everytime you watch the show, try to take away something valuable and life-affirming from it. Or, failing that, just watch and make fun of the poor shlubs who are suffering for your amusement, telling yourself that *you* would never have said something so stupid and *you* would never have pulled such a bonehead move and *you* would have sealed the deal much smoother and sooner than that loser did.

And, hey, maybe that's true. Because you've watched *Blind Date* and read and reread this invaluable and spritely written book (and bought multiple copies for all your friends and family members), maybe you won't make the same kind of mistakes as the people on the show did. And that's just one more way that *Blind Date* has made this world a happier, friendlier, more hot tub–ridden place.

But always keep in mind that for every eight or ten disasters, meltdowns, and dates from hell that you witness, there is at least one date that goes exactly as it should, ending in tenderness, warmth, and, possibly, booty. And a few—okay, *very* few—actually work out even better than that.

Acknowledgments

In the beginning, my job on *Blind Date* was very much like, well, a blind date. I walked in the door having no idea what I was getting myself into. I met my coworkers who, like 'em or not, I was going to be stuck with for a long time. And we embarked together on an adventure that would lead to some fun activities, some hilarity, a meltdown or two, and more than a few surprises, good and bad. But when we came to the end of the first date (season), it turned out that there was enough of a love connection to move on to a second and then a third.

I have met some great people during the course of *Blind Date*'s production and during the writing of this book, and I want to take this opportunity to thank them for their help and friendship.

First and most important, my deepest gratitude goes to Jason Ehrlich, who has assisted me throughout the writing of this book and who has provided a welcome harbor of sanity in the sometimes crazed world of TV production. Jason and I just happened to be crammed into the same tiny office for the second season, but—the airless, windowless atmosphere aside—it turned out to be great luck for me. Jason's going to be a major force in show business in the very near future and I'm already starting to look for the appropriate place on his coattails that I can latch onto. Thanks, Jason. I owe you big time.

And I don't see how I could have pulled through the season without the help and friendship of Michelle Wilkerson, the third member of our office trio. Admittedly, she's the coldest person in the history of the world. But beyond those blue veins and goosebumps—even in the middle of a scorching summer, I'm not kidding you—beats one of the warmest and most generous hearts in the world. She's absolutely first rate on both a personal and professional level and I'm proud and delighted to be her friend. Not to mention that without her constant encouragement and advice, I would have completed this book in half the time.

Gary Robinson was also a great friend and confidant throughout the second season. We spent a lot of time talking over projects, commiserating when things went badly, and swapping yarns and having fun when things were going well. Gary, a terrific editor, also went out of his way to help me with a video piece that I asked him to do at the very last minute. Not only did he not complain, he did a brilliant job of it. Remember the Alamo, Gary. And have a glass of Gatorade on me.

And I could never have finished this book without the help of Vincent Ly. There are times when I think Vincent is the absolute cornerstone of this show and that it would all collapse without him. Certainly, he went the extra mile for me and I appreciate it very, very much.

I also want to thank the guys who run the show, for giving me the job to begin with and then, for reasons that defy understanding, for hiring me back again and again: executive producers and co-creators Jay Renfroe, David Garfinkle, Thomas Klein, and Matthew Papish and co-executive producer Harley Tat. I really like four of you guys very much. Kidding. Come on.

And my gratitude to *Blind Date*'s incredible field producers. Not only did they produce the dates in the first place, but their notes proved invaluable to me during the writing of this book. Thanks to: Tom Romita, Diane Korman, James Gutierrez, David Suarez, and Larry Hochberg.

Thanks also to other friends who have given me so much help and support and who have all left their mark on this book: Billy Abramson, Doug Armstrong, Jim Barbee, Bill Braunstein, Chad Concelmo, James DuBose, Helen Estrada, Rick Gorman, Peter Gust, Peter Karlin, Erica Kloss, Negest Likke, Matt Odgers, Mike Palleschi, Dave Pullano, Rick Roberts, Brad Schultze, Chris Smith, and Andrew Warren.

My deepest appreciation also goes to my agent, Paul S. Levine, and, at Universal, Cindy Chang and Ned Nalle.

And I especially want to give a shout out to my pal Roger Lodge. We worked together on a regular basis without ever so much as a disagreement or harsh word. He's one of the best, both as a host and as a person, and I want to thank him for a lot of good, good times.

Finally, and most important, thanks to my wife, Claire. For everything. Literally.

About the Author

FRANK THOMPSON is an author, comedy writer, filmmaker, and film historian. His books include: *The Alamo: A Cultural History* (Taylor Publishing, 2001), *Abraham Lincoln: 20th Century Popular Portrayals* (Taylor, 1999), *AMC's Great Christmas Movies* (Taylor, 1998), *I Was That Masked Man* (Taylor, 1996, coauthor with Clayton Moore), *Lost Films* (Citadel, 1996), *The Star Film Ranch: Texas' First Picture Show* (Republic of Texas Press, 1996), *Los Angeles Uncovered* (Seaside Press, 1996), *Henry King* (Directors Guild of America, 1995), *Robert Wise: A Bio-Bibliography* (1995), *Gregory La Cava* (Filmoteca Español, 1995; coauthor), *Alamo Movies* (Republic of Texas Press, 1994), *Tim Burton's "The Nightmare Before Christmas"* (Hyperion, 1993), *Between Action and Cut: Five American Directors* (Scarecrow Press, 1985), *William A. Wellman* (Scarecrow, 1983), and others.

Thompson is currently host-producer on the hit television series *Blind Date* (Universal Television). Other television series include *Fast Food Films* (FX, 1999), *Reel Wild Cinema* (USA Network, 1996–1997), and *Hollywood Babylon* (syndicated, 1992). Thompson has written many introductory scripts for *American Movie Classics* and *Romance Classics* hosts such as Cher, Sharon Stone, Jodie Foster, Winona Ryder, Billy Bob Thornton, Martin Scorsese, Roddy McDowall, Kim Hunter, Stefanie Powers, Morgan Fairchild, Phyllis Diller, Brendan Fraser, Shirley Jones, Ali MacGraw, Kirsten Dunst, Lesley-Anne Down, Patrick Wayne, Lesley Ann Warren, Sean Young, and others. He wrote and coproduced *Frank Capra: A Personal Remembrance* (VidAmerica, 1992), and *The Making of "It's a Wonderful Life"* (Republic Pictures, 1991), both of which appear on the Republic Pictures Home Video release *It's a Wonderful Life 50th Anniversary Edition.*

Thompson wrote and directed *The Great Christmas Movies* (1998) for American Movie Classics. He served as associate producer and historical consultant, and appears onscreen, in *Wild Bill: Hollywood Maverick,* an award-winning documentary about the career of William A. Wellman (1996,

Turner Network Television). He also appears onscreen in E! Entertainment's "Louise Brooks" episode of *Mysteries and Scandals* (November 9, 1998), the History Channel documentary *The Alamo* (1996) and other cinema-related documentaries. And he appeared as a running gag on an episode of *Blind Date.*

Thompson has contributed to several film encyclopedias and is a regular writer for magazines such as *American Cinematographer, American Film, Film Comment, The Hollywood Reporter, The Disney Channel Magazine, Sight and Sound, Tower Pulse!,* and *Texas Monthly.* He has also written for many newspapers, notably the *Atlanta Journal & Constitution,* the *Miami Herald,* the *Philadelphia Inquirer,* the *San Francisco Chronicle,* the *Boston Globe,* and the *San Antonio Express News.*